"This book will be a helpful resource for many readers who want a single tool that addresses their most frequently asked questions. It will aid learner and teacher alike."

John Ortberg, senior pastor of Menlo Park Presbyterian Church,
and author of *Who Is This Man?*

"Some of the most penetrating and intriguing theological questions are the ones asked not by professional theologians but by sincere students and laypersons. Helpful answers to such questions are not, alas, as common as we might think. Thankfully, in *Theology Questions Everyone Asks*, we get some real-truth answers to go with real-life questions."

Thomas H. McCall, associate professor of biblical and systematic theology,
Trinity Evangelical Divinity School

"Don't we all have questions? I do. Not just the acceptable questions people feel comfortable asking, but the haunting questions that linger in your mind and heart; the kind of questions you may be afraid to verbalize because people will accuse you of doubt or irreverence. But these essays freely engage our questions and ask ones we have not even yet thought about. Thankfully, they also provide thoughtful answers, built on solid research and reflection, yet remaining always accessible and clear. This is a fantastic book for all who long to have their questions about the faith taken seriously."

Kelly M. Kapic, professor of theological studies, Covenant College

"*Theology Questions Everyone Asks* is exactly the kind of book needed in the undergraduate theology classroom. This text examines questions that my students ask on a regular basis and does so in a way that is engaging and relevant. The authors have done an excellent job weaving together both the biblical text and salient moments from the Christian tradition, making this book a much needed addition to the tools at hand for every undergraduate theology professor."

Mary Veeneman, assistant professor of biblical and theological studies,
North Park University

THEOLOGY

CHRISTIAN FAITH

QUESTIONS

IN PLAIN LANGUAGE

EVERYONE ASKS

Edited by
Gary M. Burge *and*
David Lauber

Foreword by
Philip G. Ryken

IVP Academic

An imprint of InterVarsity Press
Downers Grove, Illinois

InterVarsity Press
P.O. Box 1400, Downers Grove, IL 60515-1426
World Wide Web: www.ivpress.com
Email: email@ivpress.com

*InterVarsity Press® is the book-publishing division of InterVarsity Christian Fellowship/USA®, a movement of
students and faculty active on campus at hundreds of universities, colleges and schools of nursing in the United States
of America, and a member movement of the International Fellowship of Evangelical Students. For information about
local and regional activities, write Public Relations Dept., InterVarsity Christian Fellowship/USA, 6400 Schroeder
Rd., P.O. Box 7895, Madison, WI 53707-7895, or visit the IVCF website at www.intervarsity.org.*

*All Scripture quotations, unless otherwise indicated, are taken from THE HOLY BIBLE, NEW INTERNATIONAL
VERSION®, NIV® Copyright © 1973, 1978, 1984, 2011 by Biblica, Inc.™ Used by permission. All rights reserved
worldwide.*

*While all stories in this book are true, some names and identifying information in this book have been changed to
protect the privacy of the individuals involved.*

Cover design: David Fassett
Interior design: Beth Hagenberg
Image: City pedestrians: © pixalot/iStockphoto

ISBN 978-0-8308-4044-1 (print)
ISBN 978-0-8308-8448-3 (digital)

Printed in the United States of America ∞

Library of Congress Cataloging-in-Publication Data

*Theology questions everyone asks : Christian faith in plain language /
edited by Gary M. Burge and David Lauber.*

     pages cm
  Includes bibliographical references.
  ISBN 978-0-8308-4044-1 (pbk. : alk. paper)
*1. Theology, Doctrinal—Popular works. I. Burge, Gary M., 1952- editor
of compilation.*
  BT77.T44 2014
230—dc23

                                                                                   2013047716

P	21	20	19	18	17	16	15	14	13	12	11	10	9	8	7	6	5	4	3	2	1
Y	32	31	30	29	28	27	26	25	24	23	22	21	20	19	18	17	16	15	14			

CONTENTS

FOREWORD

"I have a question."

With this simple statement, a dialogue is engaged. The student asks a question; the teacher responds. The response usually raises further questions, or perhaps leaves aspects of the original question unresolved. Sometimes the teacher poses a question back to the student—a strategy that Jesus often used when people came to him with their questions. So the conversation continues, as two lively minds pass the questions and answers back and forth, enabling true learning.

The most profound questions and necessary answers are theological, pertaining to the knowledge of God. Who is God? How does he relate to the world? What are his purposes, if any, for human beings? How can we know?

College students ask these kinds of questions every day, especially the hard ones. "What is the relationship between divine sovereignty and human freedom?" they want to know, or "If God is so good, then why does he allow so much suffering?" Theodicy, soteriology, eschatology—students put all the major issues on the table. They ask personal questions, too, such as "How can I know God's will for my life?" or "After what happened, how can I ever trust God again?"

Pastors and teachers who work with college students know how hard it can be to provide answers that are theologically informed as well as biblically sound and practically beneficial. That is why I am so grateful that when students ask hard questions on my own campus they are answered by compassionate mentors who also happen to be world-class scholars. The theologians who wrote this book—friends and colleagues who teach Christian doctrine at Wheaton College—care about getting the answers right. They also care about the students who ask the questions. In this volume they offer wise and substantive answers to some of the countless questions they get asked every day in their classrooms, offices and living rooms.

These scholar-teachers know what they are talking about. Theology is one of Wheaton's most popular departments, and the contributors to this volume have won an armful of teaching awards. Many of them were educated at leading evangelical colleges and seminaries (Fuller, Moody, Trinity) before earning advanced degrees at some of the best universities in the United States (Duke, Princeton, Yale) and the United Kingdom (Aberdeen, St Andrews, Stirling).

Theology is not simply a career for these learned scholars, however; it is a way of life. As Christians who live and breathe theology every waking moment, they bring a lifetime of theological reflection to every question they face. In reading their answers, experienced pastors and trained theologians will hear unmistakable echoes of doctrinal disputes that stretched over centuries, as well as biblical principles that were defended to the point of martyrdom. But the authors wear all of this learning lightly enough to communicate clearly with contemporary college students.

The result is a remarkable model of scholarship in service to Jesus Christ, in which the best biblical, historical and systematic theology of the church speaks to the minds and hearts of a new generation. Students will read this book to *get* the answers; pastors and scholars will read this book to learn how to *give* them.

Philip G. Ryken
President
Wheaton College

CONTRIBUTORS

Vincent Bacote
Associate Professor of Theology,
Wheaton College & Graduate School
PhD, Drew University
MPhil, Drew University
MDiv, Trinity Evangelical Divinity School

Jeffrey W. Barbeau
Associate Professor of Theology,
Wheaton College & Graduate School
PhD, Marquette University
MA, Marquette University
MA, Old Dominion University

Gary M. Burge
Professor of New Testament,
Wheaton College & Graduate School
PhD, King's College, The University of Aberdeen
MDiv, Fuller Theological Seminary

Keith L. Johnson
Associate Professor of Theology,
Wheaton College & Graduate School
PhD, Princeton Theological Seminary
ThM, Duke Divinity School
MDiv, Baylor University

Beth Felker Jones
Associate Professor of Theology,
Wheaton College & Graduate School
PhD, Duke University
MTS, Duke Divinity School

George Kalantzis
Associate Professor of Theology,
Wheaton College & Graduate School
PhD, Northwestern University
MTS, Garrett-Evangelical Theological Seminary
MABS, Moody Graduate School

Timothy Larsen
Carolyn and Fred McManis Professor of Christian Thought,
Wheaton College & Graduate School
PhD, University of Stirling
MA, Wheaton College Graduate School

David Lauber
Associate Professor of Theology,
Wheaton College & Graduate School
PhD, Princeton Theological Seminary
MAR, Yale Divinity School

Gregory W. Lee
Assistant Professor of Theology,
Wheaton College & Graduate School
PhD, Duke University
MDiv, Trinity Evangelical Divinity School

Jennifer Powell McNutt
Associate Professor of Theology,
Wheaton College & Graduate School
PhD, University of St Andrews
MDiv, Princeton Theological Seminary

Daniel J. Treier

Blanchard Professor of Theology,
Wheaton College & Graduate School
PhD, Trinity Evangelical Divinity School
ThM, Grand Rapids Theological Seminary
MDiv, Grand Rapids Theological Seminary

Kevin J. Vanhoozer

Research Professor of Systematic Theology,
Trinity Evangelical Divinity School
PhD, Cambridge University
MDiv, Westminster Theological Seminary

PREFACE

The scholars in this brief volume represent over one hundred years of experience teaching introductory theology to students at both the undergraduate and graduate levels. Although each of us has taught in a number of other faculties, all but one is now teaching at Wheaton College and Graduate School.[1] At Wheaton we provide required theology courses in our general education program for undergraduates as well as graduate students. Every four years over three thousand students move through these courses. Some of our students come with extensive background; others enter these courses with minimal exposure to the great ideas that shape our faith. For them the Bible is the sole source of Christian thought and reflection on the theological discussions of the last 1,900 years. And so the creeds and the commitments of the church are an entirely new idea.

We are deeply committed to teaching these classes carefully because we are committed to our students' theological and spiritual growth. And we want them to understand why we believe what we believe. We want them to add to their devotional lives the capacity to think Christianly about the world, humanity, our redemption—myriad topics—so that in their maturity they will be able to think with agility and confidence when new questions come their way in the future.

For years we have used textbooks with great success to guide this conversation. Today we possess a rich field of books to choose from that can guide students at every level. However we have also noticed one deficit. While textbooks supply description and analysis of all the classic questions of doctrine, they often miss the *contemporary questions* our students want to ask in class. Students may wonder if the Holy Spirit is still an active force in our churches today. They may wonder whether Jesus thought about getting married. They may want to describe a current natural catastrophe and ask about God's sovereignty. Sometimes these questions are asked in class. Often they are not. And when they are asked, how often have we wondered ourselves as faculty how to frame the best answer?

This book was born out of our desire to answer those questions. As theologians, we pooled those questions we heard again and again in class, we sorted them, and we decided to answer them to the best of our ability. We did not think about this effort as a replacement for a well-written survey of Christian theology. We see it as a supplement. This is a book that can parallel any good theological text, and in it students (and faculty) can peruse the tough questions and see how we have tried to answer them. In classroom settings, this book can also be an effective discussion starter. Once the basic lecture material has been covered and students have read these contemporary questions, a stimulating classroom discussion might orbit around these lead thoughts: *Did any of these questions resonate with you? Did you find any of their answers satisfying? Unsatisfying?* The hope is that these provocative questions will "ring true" with beginning students. And when they do, their appetite and love for theology will begin to blossom. We want these questions to inspire reflection, debate and disagreement, but above all, *engagement*.

The answers to these theological questions belong to the writer of each chapter. They do not belong to Wheaton College nor does one set of answers reflect how another faculty member might approach a problem. Simply put, we are thinking aloud with the wider community of teachers and students exploring how tough questions might find creative answers. Each chapter opens with a concise summary that describes how Christian thinking has resolved some of the classic theological problems that are before us. The chapter then launches a series of specific questions and answers that follow from these problems. At the end of the book we provide a helpful list of books that will assist beginning theologians to take the next step in their study.

While we originally penned these chapters with the student in mind, we immediately recognized that we were learning from each other as well. As professors, we have heard these same questions weekly and reading the answers of our colleagues has helped our teaching. Therefore other faculty in other colleges and graduate schools may benefit just as we have, listening in as theological colleagues show their "best answers" to questions we have heard for years.

But something else occurred to us. Each of us has many years of experience teaching a variety of theological topics in the local church. And (not surprisingly) these same questions appear there. Adults (and adolescents) often have questions about their faith and yet, unlike a college, they have no curriculum or classes, and no venue where such discussions are a matter of course. And in most cases, they have no access to theology professors who can help them wrestle with many of the most challenging questions. Thus, this book could easily serve the church as well. Imagine an adult education curriculum that moves through the book each Sunday covering one chapter at a time!

So, our wider aim is to help believers—whether they be laity or students—to grow and flourish in their faith. And when an intellectual obstacle impedes that growth, we want to let them know that good and thoughtful answers are at hand that can help.

Gary Burge and David Lauber, editors
Wheaton, Illinois

1

WHAT IS CHRISTIANITY?

Timothy Larsen

Growing up I had an uncle—my mother's brother—who lived nearby our house. He was a very different kind of man from my father. Dad was a first-generation immigrant from Norway, a northerner (New Jersey), an avid reader and a businessman. My uncle, on the other hand, was a southerner (Alabama), from Scotch-Irish people who had been in the Appalachian Mountains for longer than anyone could trace, and a blue-collar outdoorsman. As a young boy, I often found my uncle's teasing, gruff way of interacting with me confusing. He had a habit of asking gotcha questions like, "What do ya know for sure?" I remember him asking me when I was about eight years old what my ethnicity was. Looking back, I suppose this was his way of trying to ferret out which side of my extended family I most identified with. I felt instinctively that it was a trick question and, searching around for a way out, pronounced triumphantly that I was "a Christian."

What does it mean to say that you are "a Christian"? The word itself is a clue as it obviously has something to do with "Christ." Christianity is a way of life that results from believing in and following Jesus Christ. Jesus of Nazareth is therefore the central figure whose life and work creates the Christian faith. During his earthly ministry, Jesus called people to himself. Those who believed in him and were willing to lay down their own priorities to follow him became his disciples. After his resurrection and ascension, his disciples gathered together in congregations. The Book of Acts tells us that "the disciples were called Christians first at Antioch" (Acts 11:26). In the early church the notion that following Christ might mean to take up one's cross and die was not just a metaphor. The earliest words after the New Testament writings that we have from a Christian woman are in the prison diary of Perpetua, who was martyred in A.D. 203. Accused by the Roman Empire of the capital crime of being a Christian, Perpetua records that her pagan father urged her to save her own life by denying her faith, but she replied to him that she could not "call myself anything else than what I am, a Christian."[1] Although those of us living in America are blessed not to face such opposition, in various regions around the world today people are still being persecuted and killed because of this confession. Christians are those who believe in Jesus Christ and follow him whatever the cost.

Isn't that setting the bar too high? After all, we are sinful and fallible people who all fall short in various ways. What is the minimum someone has to believe and do to be a Christian?

Everyone who cares about Christianity has asked themselves this question at some time or another. If you really think about it though, it is actually very weird. Imagine if I were to say to my wife: "You know, husbands are fallible people after all. So it would help me to know what is the least that I can do and what is the most I can get away with doing without you actually divorcing me. What if I never cleaned up after myself? What if I were to have an affair? What if I never said I loved you?" and so on. This would not be a healthy—perhaps not even a sane!—way to think about your marriage. The right way would be to continually wonder: what can I possibly do to make my spouse's life better and our relationship stronger? How can I be all in?

In the same way, the right way to think about the Christian faith is to ask the question: what ought a Christian to believe and do? This brings us back to the radical words of Jesus and demands of the gospel. It also leads us into full, orthodox doctrinal teaching of the faith—orthodox, after all, means "right belief." In other words, a commitment to orthodoxy calls us to not ask about the minimum necessary to believe; but rather about the correct, true beliefs in all the fullness of God's revelation to us.

It is true that we are sinful and fallible and fall short. What this means for us as individuals is that we are continually repenting of our sins and asking God for forgiveness and mercy. When we find unbelief in our hearts and minds and disobedience in our thoughts and actions, we turn to God for the grace and power to become more truly Christian. Just like when I suddenly realize that I am not speaking, feeling, thinking or acting like a good husband should, I ought not to wonder if it is nevertheless good enough to get by, but instead seek to change so that I am becoming what a good husband should be.

That is how we respond in our lives. When it comes to other people, ultimately only God is their judge. This does not mean that we have nothing to say in the face of unbelief, error, disobedience and sin. It is our duty to proclaim fully and faithfully what God has revealed, including the warnings in God's Word about the consequences for failing to respond and for persisting in sin and unbelief. Still, only God is God. We are all just God's creatures. We are like a group of elementary-school-age siblings interacting with one another. We can only report what our parents have decreed: "Dad said if you rode your bike to the park while he was gone that you would be grounded for a week." In the end, it is for the parents to decide if and when they will extend mercy. The fact that we are not the judge means that we have no right to sentence people, but only to inform them soberly of the warnings that God Almighty has given in the Bible. On the other hand, it also means that we do not have the authority to extend mercy, to enter into a plea bargain negotiation on God's behalf. It is not for us to say, for example: "Well, it is true that the Bible reveals that God has commanded us to be baptized, but I can cut you a deal and say that just believing is good enough"; or "Well, Christians have traditionally believed that Jesus rose from the dead, but as long as you believe that Jesus points the way to God then I'm content to say you are close enough and let you off on the rest if you are having a hard time buying it." Once again, the only right question to ask is: "What is the fullness of what God has commanded us to believe and do?" And the only right response is to believe it and do it and call upon others to do the same.

Is Christianity the only true religion?

The modern academic discipline of religious studies has taught people to think in terms of "religions." This approach has been criticized as a

modernist, western imposition—that western thinkers, for example, insisted that followers of Buddha or Confucius could best be thought of as
particular components of a general category called "religion" even
though this is not how they thought about it themselves. God's revelation
in the Bible does not make religion the organizing category. It tends to
ask questions along the lines of: Is this a true or false way to think and
speak about God? Is this a faithful or unfaithful way to worship God?
Are there signs of God's grace at work here?

In other words, Christians should usually resist thinking of following
Jesus as a religion. That might be how it looks from the outside by a religious studies scholar who does not believe that Jesus is the Son of God,
but it is not how it looks to a believer. The theologian Karl Barth spoke
of religion as humanity's faulty attempts to try to understand God on
their own, while Jesus Christ is God's self-disclosing revelation. Dietrich
Bonhoeffer therefore sought to underline this distinction by speaking of
rejecting religion but not the Christian faith. He called it "religionless
Christianity."[2] This idea has caught on with many Christians today (although its popular form is a far cry from the profound views of Barth
and Bonhoeffer). For example, at the time of writing this, Jefferson
Bethke, an evangelist from Mark Driscoll's Mars Hill Church in Seattle,
has a YouTube video that has gone viral (currently at 26 million views),
"Why I Hate Religion, but Love Jesus."[3]

We are back to our need to proclaim the gospel truth fully and faithfully, without being so presumptuous as to pretend to sit in the judgment
seat. The judgment of specific individuals—whether they call themselves
Muslim or Mormon, Baptist or Buddhist, Anglican or Atheist, or anything else—is God's call alone. What we are called to do is share the good
news of the gospel. We are neither authorized to cut deals for those who
reject parts of it nor to pronounce a sentence upon them. God is the God
of all people and the judge of all the earth, and he will do what is right.

**But if there was no religion, wouldn't that put an end to a lot of
violence and make for a more tolerant, peaceful world?**

The idea that getting rid of religion would get rid of a lot of human violence is a myth. The Soviet Union was officially opposed to religion and

got rid of it as far as it possibly could, but it was still one of the most oppressive, bloody states—counting the lives of its own people very cheap and slaughtering them in horrific numbers, as well as being willing to ferment violence around the world. This sad tale has been true of other anti-religion states as well and still is in some places today. North Korea has certainly not become a more tolerant, less violent part of the world by deciding to get rid of religion.

We have already mentioned that religion is itself not usually a helpful way to conceptualize realities. Still, it is one way of labeling what people care about most, where people find meaning in life. Everything that people care deeply about they tend to find worth fighting for. Consider "crimes of passion," where, for example, someone's deep love for another leads to jealousy and then the murder of a rival. Saying that we would have less violence if we did not have religion is like saying we would have less violence if people never fell in love. I suppose on one level that might be strictly true, but it would just be another way of saying that if human beings did not care about things that matter to them then they would not fight over them. Its potential to cause violence is not an argument against religion any more than it is an argument against love or family or anything else that can be the occasion for conflict. Religion, like romantic love and family, is one of the things that makes human life meaningful and precious.

Moreover, how can you get people to behave violently? Or to justify their own brutal acts to themselves? One of the most effective ways is to appeal to what they care about most. Samuel Johnson once famously and sagely remarked, "Patriotism is the last refuge of a scoundrel." That is to say, it is precisely because good people rightly have a love of country that a bad person will appeal to this value in order to manipulate the situation for evil ends. Patriotic reasons are presented because love of country is good, but they mask baser motives when appealed to by a scoundrel. This has often happened with the Christian faith throughout history. For example, plantation owners in the first half of the nineteenth century might have quoted the Bible in order to justify enslaving people and whipping them, but this was a way to rationalize their own economic self-interest and selfish desires. If there was no religion, it would not mean that violence and injustice would have gone away but only that exploiters would have found another reason. They would have said it was for the good of their country or their family or whatever else could be twisted to give some ostensibly respectable cover to their actions. It is not religion that causes violence but rather it is the dearness of faith to the hearts of people that causes wicked people to exploit it for evil ends.

In fact, the force of this question can be completely reversed. As a Christian, I have faith that Jesus Christ, the Prince of Peace, will someday put an end to all violence—that there will come a day when there is no more "death or mourning or crying or pain" (Revelation 21:4). After the failure of communism, it no longer seems that there are atheists who have any utopian hopes that human beings will someday become a harmonious race where everyone is cooperating with and helping one another. In fact, if they thought about it, atheists would likely have to admit that they expect violence to end only with the extinction of the human race. Thus, the Christian faith is not the cause of violence, but rather our source of hope that it will be overcome.

Does secularization mean that Christianity is destined to die out as society becomes more modern?

This is another myth. It originally got traction through the ideas of atheistic intellectuals in the nineteenth century. The French philosopher Auguste Comte claimed to have discovered a law that humanity progresses through three stages: the religious, the metaphysical and the scientific. This was a way of claiming that religion was a primitive way of thinking from the infancy of the race and that it was destined to die off and be completely replaced by scientific thinking. Various other leading agnostic thinkers claimed something similar. Marx and Freud both presented belief in God as an illusion that humanity was finally learning to dispense with. These figures were merely expressing what they, as people who did not believe in God themselves, *wished* would happen. As it had not happened already, their statements about the development of human society were really prophecies. Ironically, they were also deeply unscientific assertions. Despite lauding the scientific as the destiny of humanity, Comte clearly had no idea how real scientists go about finding warrant for and formulating a law. Freud has also been shown to be very unscientific in the way he went about constructing his views—and Marx's predictions about how society would develop have been proven false on multiple fronts.

Still, this mythology led many people to imagine that modern thought was disproving belief in God and therefore that thinking, educated people would no longer find it possible to believe. For some people this probably even became a self-fulfilling prophecy—worrying that they would be "left behind," as it were, when thinking people stopped going to church to make sure that they were keeping up with where they imagined the world was going.

Things did not develop as the great nineteenth-century agnostic thinkers imagined, however. In the twentieth century a lot of leading intellectuals were actually Christians; quite a few of them even returned to faith as mature thinkers or came to faith later in life. Today there are numerous leading philosophers, scientists, novelists, artists, politicians, academics and intellectuals who are very open about their Christian faith. In fact, recent studies have shown that people with more education—particularly at least one college degree—are more likely to go to church than less well-educated people, the exact opposite of what people like Freud imagined would happen.

With those predications not working out, a second version of secularization theory arose in the twentieth century. In this view, religion would not die out because of an intellectual defeat but rather through sociological changes. Modern society, with its factors such as urbanization, industrialization and individualism, was said to be incompatible with faith and therefore religion was destined to wither away as culture became more modern. This view was particularly fashionable in western Europe where declining church membership and attendance seemed to lend proof to it. There was one problem, however. The United States of America was generally leading the world in technological advance and modernization, and yet faith was not diminishing there the way it was in places like England or Sweden. This led some sociologists to speak of "American exceptionalism"—that the United States was an anomaly. In the twenty-first century, however, it has become increasingly clear that religion has a great deal of vitality in most parts of the world. If strong spiritual beliefs and practices mark the lives of billions of people across Africa, Asia and Latin America, then maybe what needs to be explained is "European exceptionalism"—religion is normal in the contemporary world and therefore its torpid state in Europe is what needs a special explanation to account for it. The Christian faith has been rapidly growing even in historically non-Christian countries such as China. Similarly, although no one could justly claim that it is a less modern or advanced society than others, Christianity has made amazing advances in South Korea in recent decades.

This does not mean that we should become complacent about the health of Christianity in the future. Christians are followers of Jesus Christ and our Master rattles us out of any such complacency with his probing question: "When the Son of Man comes, will he find faith on the earth?" (Luke 18:8). Perhaps part of the reason he said that was to keep us alert enough to prevent us from being bullied out of our beliefs by false prophets who declare that belief in God is destined to die out in the modern world.

Christianity Worldwide. About one-third of the world's population identifies as Christian today. In 1910, only about 9% of Africans were Christians; today almost half of all Africans self-identify as Christians. In the first decade of the twenty-first century, Africa had the fastest growth rate for Christianity, while Europe had the slowest. In 1910, 66% of the world's Christians were in Europe; today it is only 25%. The majority of the world's Christians today are not in the West, but in Africa, Asia and Latin America. There are more evangelical Christians in China today than there are in the United States, more in India than in Great Britain. South Korea now sends out more Christian missionaries than Great Britain or Germany. India now sends out more Christian missionaries than Canada. There are around 707 million evangelical Christians in the world today.[4]

But hasn't Christianity always been opposed to scientific advances? What about Galileo and all that?

This is also a misconception. Modern science arose within Christian societies and Christian beliefs, habits, commitments and interests made it possible. Many of the greatest scientists in the past have been devout Christians (Sir Isaac Newton, for instance) and this is still true today. The idea that faith and science are at odds with each other was actually created by agnostic scientists as a way to attack Christianity. The only problem was that this picture was not accurate. In fact, many urban legends were created. (That is my polite way of saying that they were telling lies!) For example, agnostic scientists claimed that Christians taught that the world was flat and opposed the view that it is round. Actually, the Greeks and Romans knew that the world was round before the time of Christ and Christians never thought the world was flat. Even in the midst of the so-called Dark Ages a monk like the Venerable Bede (d. 735) knew and taught that the world was round, as did the theologians of the medieval church and beyond. And there are many such urban legends.

It is true that Galileo's ideas about the nature of the solar system were investigated and condemned by the Inquisition. This historical detail does not teach us that Christianity is typically opposed to scientific advances, however. What it really tells us is that the medieval Inquisition was a power-hungry, control-freak, oppressive institution. It was terribly afraid of anything it did not understand or could not control and was quick to use force to suppress it. This is a classic example of a corrupt institution, an abuse of power and of unchristian things being done in the name of Christ. But it is not about a Christian campaign against science. In fact, far more saints than scientists were persecuted by the Inquisition. Joan of Arc, for example, was condemned as a heretic and burned at the stake (Galileo was merely confined to house arrest). Since her death, Joan of Arc has been formally canonized by the Roman Catholic Church and is now one of the most popular and beloved of saints. There are many lessons to learn from this dark chapter of church history, but the idea that the Christian faith and modern science are inherently in conflict is not one of them.

The Faith vs. Science Myth. The idea that the Christian faith is opposed to scientific advance was made popular by two books, John William Draper, *History of the Conflict between Religion and Science* (1874) and Andrew Dickson White, *A History of the Warfare of Science with Theology in Christendom* (1896). Although these books pretended to be documenting a conflict between faith and science, they were actually trying to create one. They did this by presenting as "facts" many urban legends and false claims. For example, they both claimed that the church opposed the use of anesthetics for expectant mothers during labor on the grounds that it was a violation of the statement in Genesis that childbirth would be painful. This was simply made up. No church opposed anesthetics. Instead, the inventor of chloroform received fan mail from ministers from all the major denominations thanking him for helping to alleviate the suffering of women in labor.

Why are there so many different Christian denominations?

Jesus prayed that his disciples "may be one" (John 17:21) and therefore we know that the unity of the church, of believers, is God's will. All Christians should be grieved by division in the body of Christ and work toward unity. It is not clear, however, that Jesus desired for the church to be united through a single institutional structure with a human leader at the top. This is the Roman Catholic view—that all Christians should find their unity under the leadership of the bishop of Rome, the Pope. The eastern churches such as Greek and Russian Orthodoxy, however, only envision a single, hierarchal, institutional church across a single group of people or national bloc, and with the various churches existing in doctrinal agreement and fellowship with one another but with no human authority at the top of them all. Many Protestants—of which I am one—believe that the unity Jesus prayed for is a unity of doctrine, fellowship and the Spirit, but not necessarily a unity of institutional organization and human chain of command and authority. If this view is right, then the existence of different denominations would not be inherently a mark of disunity—they could be a way for God's people to come together in manageable, relational networks of local congregations which are also in core doctrinal unity and the unity of the Spirit and fellowship with other networks. This is not the current state of the church, however, and therefore if we are honest we must admit that we are in a state of disunity which grieves the Holy Spirit.

It would be wrong therefore to try to justify our denominationalism as it currently exists, complete with differences of doctrine on vital points and even sometimes a lack of goodwill between some groups, let alone a lack of unity in the Spirit. Nevertheless, just as violence *per se* should not be justified, though it can be a sign that something worth fighting for is at stake, so the many denominations not in full fellowship with one another are partially an unfortunate byproduct of good desires. Christians rightly desire to take their stand on key points of doctrine and practice that they believe faithfulness to God requires even at the price of setting them apart from others. The unity Jesus prayed for is not that Christians would be so careless and apathetic about their beliefs, worship and manner of life that they would join with others on any terms. True unity will only come as all believers draw closer to the center who is Christ in faithfulness, obedience, charity, selflessness, grace and truth.

What is meant by evangelicalism?

For many people in America today, "evangelical" probably conjures up an image of an angry, white, male brandishing a political poster. A truer mental picture of an evangelical would be an African, Asian or Latin American woman smiling and swaying as she joyfully sings praises to God. Evangelicalism is a truly global expression of Christianity. The main action of the story today is often in the Majority World.

The evangelical movement began in Protestant groups in the first half of the eighteenth century. They had become concerned that while people might give lip service to God and to Christian doctrine, they had not really been transformed by the power of the gospel. They might know about God, but they did not actually know God. They began to long for revival and renewal to come and for people to become truly spiritually alive in Christ. Soon they came to realize that they had more in common with Christians from other denominations that also felt this way than they did with people in their own denomination who did not. The root word for "evangelical" is *gospel* and therefore they started referring to people like themselves as "evangelicals"—those people who prioritized the message of the gospel and its effectiveness to transform people's lives. To say that someone was, like you, also an Anglican or a Baptist or a Presbyterian was only to say that they agreed with you on certain points of doctrine or church order. That counts for little, however, if they are only a nominal Christian with no living relationship with Jesus Christ. To say that they are an "evangelical," on the other hand, was a way of saying: "They might be a Presbyterian, while I'm a Baptist, but I know that we both agree on the good news of the atoning death and resurrection of Jesus Christ and the importance of people being converted by its saving power—that we share a common testimony of this work of God in our lives—and that is more important than our differences."

Evangelicals are Christians who believe in the gospel, a message which has at its heart the work of Christ, the Son of God incarnate, on the cross on our behalf. They believe that this is good news for all people and that Christians are called to join in the great task of working for all people to hear it—that is, the work of evangelism and missions. They believe in the power of the Holy Spirit to bring conversion and then an ongoing life of fellowship with God and empowerment to love and serve others and to live God's way. They believe in the Bible as the unique source of God's word written and the final authority God has given us in matters of faith and practice.

It is because evangelicals believe they are called to spread the gospel that so many Christians from western countries went to other parts of the world as missionaries in the nineteenth and twentieth centuries. This was, in a sense, only to return the favor, as both Britain and Germany were once pagan countries in need of foreign missionaries to bring them the good news of Jesus Christ. So westerners went to the world in the 1800s and 1900s. It is partially the seeds they planted then that are now producing such a harvest of vibrant Christian faith in Africa, Latin America and Asia. Evangelicalism is readily adaptable to many different contexts. Believers with Bibles empowered by the Spirit quickly turn into churches, spreading the gospel and planting more churches. The mission fields of the past then become the missionary-sending places of the present. For example, many Christian missionaries today are being sent *from* South Korea, a place they were being sent *to* a hundred years ago.

Defining Evangelicalism. Here is a definition that I developed to help people understand what is meant by evangelicalism. An evangelical is

- a Protestant orthodox Christian
- who stands in the tradition of the global Christian networks arising from the eighteenth-century revival movements associated with John Wesley and George Whitefield
- who has a preeminent place for the Bible in her or his Christian life as the divinely inspired, final authority in matters of faith and practice
- who stresses reconciliation with God through the atoning work of Jesus Christ on the cross
- and who stresses the work of the Holy Spirit in the life of an individual to bring about conversion and an ongoing life of fellowship with God and service to God and others, including the duty of all believers to participate in the task of proclaiming the gospel to all people.

2

WHAT IS THE BIBLE?

Kevin J. Vanhoozer

For over twenty-five years I have sought to answer the question "What does it mean to be biblical?" Why would anyone devote half of his or her life to that question, especially when all one has to do is look up the dictionary definition ("relating to or contained in the Bible")? The reason why is that answering this question is tied up with two other, even more important questions: Jesus' "Who do you say that I am?" and Bonhoeffer's "Who is Jesus Christ for us today?" In short: I am interested in what it means to be biblical because being biblical is part and parcel of being a disciple of Jesus Christ. The Bible is a book that leads to Jesus and helps disciples to follow in his way.

The Bible is not a single book but a library—a collection of sixty-six texts written by diverse authors who lived centuries apart in a variety of literary forms that nevertheless point to, and help explain, what God was doing in the history of Israel and then Jesus Christ to reconcile the world to himself (2 Corinthians 5:19).

The Bible is a two-storied library, though all the books on both floors ultimately tell a single story. On the ground floor, the Old Testament (from Latin *testamentum* meaning "covenant") tells the story of the covenant God made with the people of ancient Israel at Mount Sinai after he had brought them out of captivity in Egypt (Exodus 19–31). Books on the second floor tell the story of a new covenant that God made with both Jews and non-Jews (that is, *Gentiles*) on the basis not of ethnicity but rather faith in Jesus Christ.

The Bible is therefore not one thing. To present-day Jews, the Old

Testament alone is sacred Scripture. To present-day Christians, the Old and New Testaments together make up the Bible. To historians, the Bible provides evidence with which to critically reconstruct the religious history and cultural development of ancient Near Eastern peoples and cultures, especially ancient Israel and the early church. To others, the Bible is an example of religious literature, to be appreciated not as evidence but as a compelling imaginative narrative. People of faith, however, accept the Bible "not as a human word but as what it really is, God's word" (1 Thessalonians 2:13 NRSV). From the perspective of historic Christian faith, the Bible is Holy Scripture: the divinely inspired account of God's will for humanity (law) and an authoritative transcript of God's covenant-making initiatives for the salvation of the world (grace). In order to do full justice to what the Bible is, one must recognize its historical, literary and theological character. In the first place, the Bible is the work of human authors whose writings have historical occasions and reflect the prevailing cultural forms. It is human discourse: something someone said about something in writing to someone, in some way, for some purpose. Yet it is also divine discourse: God is the ultimate author, saying something by means of what the humans say. The technical term is revelation: God reveals himself or makes himself known through the discourse of his prophets (Hebrews 1:1) and apostles.

The Bible is therefore a form of divine address, the means by which God speaks to his people: *verbal* revelation, the proclamation of the gospel, the good news that God reigns, that his kingdom has come in Jesus Christ, and that through Christ God has made things right. Only speech renders behavior unambiguous: we would not know God or what God was doing unless we had actual words from God. And this is precisely what we see happening in Scripture. God speaks in order to make himself and his intentions known. God speaks to Adam in the garden of Eden. God makes covenants with Abraham (Genesis 12; 15; 17). God speaks to Moses out of the burning bush (Exodus 3:14) and to the whole nation of Israel from Mt. Sinai (Exodus 19–20).

God makes himself known through Scripture and establishes relationships with those who respond to his word in faith. The Bible does much more than communicate information: it mediates a personal relationship with God. For God can do many things with words: inform, command, promise, narrate, warn, exhort, console, justify, even transform minds and renew hearts. Above all, God can use the human words of the Bible to direct people to Jesus Christ, the eternal Word of God made flesh, the promise of salvation made good.

The Bible is a big book. That is because it answers the big questions of life—why are we here? what should we be doing? where are we going?—by showing how both the origin and the destiny of the universe, and humanity, are connected to God's eternal plan to extend his nuclear family (such as the fellowship of the triune God in himself) by creating and then uniting all things to his Son, Christ Jesus (Colossians 1:15-20). The Bible is a big book containing a variety of communications (stories, laws, prophecies, letters, songs), all of which are intended to bring its community of readers into covenantal relationship, and hence communion, with God and one another. Being biblical means understanding and responding rightly to God's various communications in the Bible.

Do Christians need to read the Old Testament?

This is hardly a new question. One of the earliest controversies in the early church was over the extent to which Christians had to abide by the religion, such as the temple sacrifices, and practices, such as circumcision, of the Jews (Acts 15). The "Judaizers" in the early church (early Christians who believed that they had to preserve Jewish religious traditions) taught strict adherence to the Old Testament. But it would be a mistake to think that their opponents, notably the apostle Paul, dismissed the Old Testament altogether in their attempts to clarify the status of the Law and its demands. There are at least four reasons why Christians need not only to read the Old Testament, but also to acknowledge its proper authority.

First, we do not want to repeat the mistake of Marcion, a second-century church bishop (later excommunicated), who thought the Old Testament Scriptures were inferior because the *God* of the Old Testament was inferior to the *God* of the New Testament. Marcion sounds remarkably contemporary when he contrasts the loving Father God of Jesus and the New Testament with the wrathful deity of the Old Testament, a jealous tribal deity whose occasional actions, most notably genocide, made him no better than a moral monster. In refusing to acknowledge that the God of the New Testament is the same as the God of the Old Testament, Marcion failed to identify God correctly and threatened to tear asunder what God has put together: the work of creation and the work of redemption. Marcion failed to appreciate the compassion of God in the Old Testament (see, for example, Exodus 34:6-7, and its repetition in Nehemiah 9:17; Psalm 86:15; Jonah 4:2; Joel 2:13) and the wrath of God in the New (see, for example, Romans 1:18; Ephesians 5:6; Colossians 3:6; Revelation 19:15).

Second, both Jesus and the gospel are ultimately unintelligible apart from the Old Testament. The point of the Bible is to communicate God's loving plan for the salvation of the world, and Jesus' place in the plan makes no sense unless we first know something about creation itself, the fall of creation into the captivity of sin and death, and the covenantal promises of God to make things right (Romans 1:2). John Calvin rightly saw that the Old Testament had a pedagogical function: it teaches us of our need for Christ (we cannot fulfill all righteousness by keeping the law ourselves) and it shows us the gracious provision God has made (that is, bloody sacrifices that atone for sin) to satisfy his need to do what is right (that is, execute justice) without destroying the unrighteous. Both Testaments, we might say, preach Christ, though the Old Testament points forward to the New and the New Testament refers back to the Old.

Third, and following from the above: the New Testament is ultimately unintelligible apart from the Old Testament. About ten percent of the New Testament consists of quotations, paraphrases and allusions to the Old Testament. Without knowledge of the Old Testament, much of what transpires in the New is simply baffling. Much in Jesus' life and death, for example, happened in order to fulfill Old Testament prophecy (see, for example, Matthew 21:4). Indeed, the very thrust of the New Testament—that God has, through Christ, fulfilled his promises to Israel—is unintelligible apart from a knowledge of God's prior words and deeds recorded in the Old Testament.

Fourth, and finally: Christians should have the same attitude towards the Old Testament as did Jesus himself. Christians believe the Bible because they believe in Christ. Jesus repeatedly cites books from the Old

Testament as having authority: "It is written" carries the connotation "authoritative because God says so." In his controversies with the Pharisees, Jesus never questioned their appeal to Scripture, only their way of interpreting it: "You search the Scriptures because you think that in them you have eternal life; and it is they that bear witness about me" (John 5:39 ESV).

Who decided which books belong in the Bible and how do we know they were right?

There are many aspects to this important question. First, why should we think that books written by different people at different times and in different genres have something in common? Second, how do we know which books belong in the Bible if the Bible itself does not give us a list? Third, should we believe contemporary skeptics who say that the list of books in our Bible simply reflects the interests of the faction that wielded the most power in the early church?

For a while, Christians could more or less afford to neglect these problems, because there was a general consensus on which books were part of the authoritative collection. However, though there is an overlap, Orthodox, Protestants and Roman Catholics work with different lists. (Roman Catholics include "apocryphal" books written by Jews in the four-hundred-year gap between the Old and New Testaments. Orthodox Christians have the same list of New Testament books as Protestants and Roman Catholics but follow the Septuagint, the Greek translation of the Hebrew Scriptures, as the basis for their larger list of Old Testament books.) The problem of what books make up the Bible has become even more exacerbated in recent times with the 1945 discovery of other ancient texts, like the *Gospel of Thomas*, which is not part of the New Testament, though it is composed of sayings attributed to Jesus—one hundred and fourteen of them! Faced with such evidence, some scholars suggest that the list of which books belong in the Bible was simply an accident of history: the Bible's table of contents simply reflects which faction in the early church won the power struggle to decide orthodoxy, as Dan Brown suggests in his best-selling novel (and film) *The Da Vinci Code*.

All these developments have made the canon (from Greek *kanon* =

"measuring rod" or "rule") an urgent question, especially for those churches that are heirs of the Reformation and hold to the supreme authority of Scripture, and cannot therefore simply appeal to what the Vatican or some other body has decided about what or what not to include. D. F. Strauss, a nineteenth century New Testament historian, calls the question of the canon the "Achilles' heel" of Protestant Christianity. As we shall see, however, Protestant Christians are not entirely without means to answer the question, "Why just *these* books?" Everything depends on how one views the nature of the canon together with its relationship to God and the people of God. The so-called Muratorian fragment, an excerpt from a seventh-century copy of what scholars think may be one of the oldest lists of New Testament books, mentions all the writings in the New Testament with the exception of Hebrews, 1 and 2 Peter, James and 3 John. It explicitly rejects an Epistle to the Laodiceans as a forgery, and accepts the second-century book *The Shepherd of Hermas* as appropriate for private but not public reading. All twenty-seven New Testament books are accepted as canonical in Athanasius's Easter Letter of A.D. 367. Orthodox, Roman Catholics and Protestants agree that the books on this list are canonical (though the first two groups supplement the list with other books). The story of how the church came to recognize the various books of the Bible as worthy of inclusion in the canon is well documented. The remaining question, however, is how we should explain this story. What reasons do Christians *today* have for continuing to give a special authoritative status to just these books?

One strategy for answering this question is to demonstrate that the biblical books were written either by prophets or apostles. Such historical accounts are valuable, though the evidence is contested, and so the best one can hope for is a degree of probability. Another approach is the "community determined" model. This model explains the canon in terms of the process of canonization: the reception in and recognition by the community as authoritative. The problem with this account is that there are rival communities (e.g., Protestant vs. Roman Catholic). Though the canon has a "natural history," we need more than history fully to account for what the canon is. Christians confess the Bible to be God's word, hence an appeal to theology (i.e., God) to understand the canon is both necessary and fitting. Let me make four points.

1. The theological principle that God will explain what he's up to leads us to expect that revelatory words will accompany redemptive deeds (so Herman Ridderbos, a New Testament scholar). Indeed, this is what we find in both the Old and New Testaments. When God acts to save, he speaks to inform, or instructs others (prophets, apostles) to speak on his behalf. One advantage to this idea is that it explains why the canon is closed: the once-for-allness of the canon derives from the once-for-allness of Jesus Christ (Hebrews 9:12, 26; 10:10).

2. The Bible clearly depicts God as speaking to his people and, on occasion, making his word permanent by instructing it to be written down. For example, the Ten Commandments were written on stone and then placed in the Ark of the Covenant. God's word is holy because it is set apart, and this is precisely what the canon does: its sets off just these texts as God's authoritative word, intended to regulate the life of his people.

3. The Bible clearly depicts God as making covenants with his people. One of the elements of these ancient covenants was a provision for making permanent copies, standing witnesses as it were to the agreement. The whole book of Deuteronomy is such a covenant and, significantly, includes a mandate not to change a single word: "You must neither add anything to what I command you nor take away anything from it, but keep the commandments of the LORD your God with which I am charging you" (Deuteronomy 4:2 NRSV; see also 12:32). The suggestion here is that "canon" is a covenant document, the constitution as it were of the covenant people.

4. The three previous points help to explain the concept of the canon, but they do not yet explain why we have *just these books*. The short answer is that *just these texts* are the ones appointed by the risen Christ to be the human vehicles of his voice: "My sheep hear my voice . . . and they follow me" (John 10:27 NRSV). Christians believe that only when the Holy Spirit opens their eyes and ears can they see and hear the Bible for what it is (compare Romans 8:16). The church is indeed involved in the formation of the canon, but viewed theologically, the church's role is that of following the Spirit's prompts: the church does not create the canon

but confesses its divine authorship. In sum, we can say that the canon is the Rule of Christ: the authoritative answer to the Lord's question ("Who do you say that I am?"), the norm to which everything else we say about God and the gospel has to measure up and the means through which the risen Christ now rules his church.

Athanasius's 39th Festal (Easter) Letter (A.D. 367). The first canonical list that matches all twenty-seven books in our New Testament comes from a letter written by Athanasius, bishop of Alexandria, in the fourth century. This does not mean that the church did not have a Bible for four centuries, only that it took that long for the various churches, separated by geography and language, to come to a consensus on which books were genuine, to be accepted by all, and which were spurious. Here is Athanasius on the books of the New Testament: "These are the four Gospels, according to Matthew, Mark, Luke, and John. Afterwards, the Acts of the Apostles and Epistles (called Catholic), seven, namely of James, one; of Peter, two; of John, three; after these, one of Jude. In addition, there are fourteen Epistles of Paul, written in this order. The first, to the Romans; then two to the Corinthians; after these, to the Galatians; next, to the Ephesians; then to the Philippians; then to the Colossians; after these, two to the Thessalonians, and that to the Hebrews; and again, two to Timothy; one to Titus; and lastly, that to Philemon. And besides, the Revelation of John." The Council of Carthage officially approved Athanasius's list in A.D. 397.[1]

How can the Bible be both God's Word and Matthew's word (not to mention Mark, Luke and John)?

Why, after the public reading of a Bible passage in many churches, does the reader say "The word of the Lord" and the congregation respond "Thanks be to God"? What about the rights of the human authors? Who holds the copyright to the Bible? The Westminster Confession of Faith

(1646) is typical of Protestant statements on the matter: "The authority of the Holy Scripture, for which it ought to be believed, and obeyed, depends not upon the testimony of any man, or Church; but wholly upon God (who is truth itself) the author thereof."[2] Lurking behind this familiar association of the Bible with God's Word, however, lies one of the most challenging theological problems: the relationship of divine sovereignty and human freedom; the manner in which individual events are jointly caused by God and human beings.

The issue in question is inspiration: "All Scripture is breathed out [*theopneustos*, "inspired"] by God" (2 Timothy 3:16 ESV). If Jesus Christ is the Word of God, the Holy Spirit is the breath that carries it: "no prophecy of Scripture is a matter of one's own interpretation, because no prophecy ever came by human will, but men and women moved by the Holy Spirit spoke from God" (2 Peter 1:20-21 NRSV). These two passages give us important metaphors to guide our thinking about God's authorship, but neither could be said to provide a full-blown theory of inspiration. That has not stopped theologians from offering suggestions.

There are three inadequate views. (1) Some see inspiration as pertaining to the *individual human authors* themselves, but this proves either too little or too much. According to the model of "ecstatic prophecy," the human person is simply a mouthpiece for God. This does not give enough weight to genuine human authorship and so falls prey to the dictation view. Alternately, to say that the authors were inspired, rather than their texts, is to relocate inspiration away from the biblical words themselves. (2) Some view the Spirit's influence as affecting the *thoughts*, but not the words, of the human authors. This too fails to preserve dual authorship because, first, it is not clear how God can ensure that the right words be freely chosen to express the divine thoughts (thus calling into question the reality of divine authorship). And second, it appears simply to push the problem of divine dictation back one step (thus calling into question the integrity of human authorship). (3) Some see inspiration as referring to the Bible's effect on its *readers*, the way a good teacher inspires her students. However, this view fails to account for the unique relationship of God to Scripture, and trades more on the English term *inspired* than it does the key term in 2 Timothy 3:16 (*theo-*

pneustos = God-breathed), which suggests that inspiration has to do with what comes out of God's mouth (that is, words).

The traditional view, represented by both Luther and Calvin, is that God inspired the very words of the Bible, but not in such a way as to overpower the human authors or override their human faculties. Luther thought that knowing Hebrew and Greek was important because it was in these two languages that the Holy Spirit wrote the Old and New Testaments. Calvin agreed, only adding that when God speaks to human beings, he has to "lisp," as nurses commonly do with infants. All of this, though, would seem to avoid the more central question: how can the very words of the Bible be fully God's and fully the human authors'?

It was the lie of the serpent to portray God's reign as oppressive and tyrannical. Divine sovereignty and human freedom do not add up to a zero-sum game. Some theologians view verbal inspiration as a special case of divine providence, in which divine and human authorship are compatible with one another. God so shapes the individual personalities and histories of each biblical author that he freely writes just what God wills to be written. Others appeal to the sanctifying work of the Holy Spirit. B. B. Warfield, the great theologian of old Princeton (1887–1921) and author of a classic study of biblical authority and inspiration, goes further, arguing that inspiration is not an example of general providence but an extraordinary influence of the Holy Spirit, who did not merely sanctify but supernaturally guided the process of writing, effectually prompting the authors freely to write the very words of God.[3] This is close to what the Dutch theologian Herman Bavinck, Warfield's contemporary and peer, calls the "organic" view of inspiration that insists God speaks through human authors even as they remain their own speaking and thinking (that is, cooperating) subjects.[4] The prophets spoke on God's behalf and at God's behest: "Thus saith the Lord." Verbal inspiration is ultimately about the finished product; the actual process remains a mystery.

Still others try to resolve the tension between divine and human authorship by drawing a comparison between Jesus' incarnation and the Bible's "inscripturation." Just as Jesus had a divine and human nature, so too does Scripture. While popular, this analogy is seriously misleading.

Christology refers to two natures in *one* person; Scripture pertains to one discourse with *two* speech agents. The Bible does not have a divine and human nature but divine and human *authors*.

Christ is, however, the clue to the way forward. The prophets were God's commissioned speakers who spoke ultimately of Christ (Luke 24:27). The apostles were Christ's own commissioned spokesmen. They spoke on Christ's behalf, about Christ, through Christ's Spirit, whom he had promised would guide them into all truth (John 16:13-14). It is ultimately the Spirit of Christ speaking in the Scriptures, through the prophets and apostles (1 Peter 1:10-11). And the Spirit of Jesus Christ does not work against human freedom but establishes it, organically: "I can do all things [even convey God's word] through him who strengthens me" (Philippians 4:13 ESV).

Sola Scriptura. This famous slogan states the formal principle of the Protestant Reformation: "Scripture alone" is the supreme authority for Christian faith, life and thought. With the other *solas* (that is, faith alone, grace alone, Christ alone, glory to God alone), *sola scriptura* marks the Reformers' attempt to restore supremacy in the church to God alone. However, *sola scriptura* does not mean *"solo" scriptura*: it is not so much that the Bible is the sole source of theology (it isn't) but rather that the Bible alone is the supreme criterion of theology. In other words, *sola scriptura* does not mandate that Christians read the Bible with no help from any other source, only that Scripture alone is supremely authoritative. *Sola scriptura* is not opposed to church tradition, then, though it does insist that tradition is ultimately subordinate to Scripture. The Spirit speaking in the Scriptures has magisterial authority, but the Spirit guiding church tradition exercises ministerial authority. God's word in Scripture serves as a light unto our path, yet tradition is to Scripture as the moon is to the sun. Tradition is the refracted light that enables the church to follow the path all through the night.

May I read the Bible like any other book, the Gospel of John like John Irving?

As we have just seen, God speaks by means of human authors. What these human authors wrote reflects the language and culture of their respective historical times. They wrote not only in the language but also in the literary styles of the day. It often helps to know something about the historical background and context of the author, and about the possible meanings (called the *semantic range*) Hebrew and Greek words had at the time the author used them.

Whether we're reading the Gospel of John or John Irving's *A Prayer for Owen Meany*, we want to grasp what authors are saying and doing in and with their texts. Interpreters want to understand what the author means or communicates, namely, the author's *discourse*: what someone said in some way at some time to someone for some purpose. To a certain extent, then, we read the Bible as we do other texts: we try to grasp what authors have said and done by paying attention to the way their words go, and we do this by attending to grammar, historical context, and literary genre.

This analogy (reading the Bible like any other book) is marked, however, by an even greater dissimilarity, for no other book is authored by God, centered on Christ, and illumined by the Holy Spirit as is the Bible. It is important to acknowledge that God is doing things with the words of Scripture beyond (but not opposed) to what the human authors can do. To read the Bible as divine discourse is to read the parts in light of the whole, for ultimately the canon as a whole is a unified divine work. This is why "Scripture interprets Scripture" is such an important interpretive principle.

There are ways to read the Bible that are *unlike* the way we read other books. First, we ought to read the Bible in a spirit of prayer and humility, acknowledging that our minds are darkened and in need of the illumination of word and Spirit. Second, we ought to read the Bible as a word that is ultimately from Christ (John 16:13-15; Revelation 1:1-2), about Christ (John 5:39-40; Luke 24:25-27), and intended to form in us the mind of Christ (1 Corinthians 2:16; Philippians 2:5). Finally, we ought to read the Bible in a spirit of trust, confident that even the difficult parts will eventually cast a light onto our path (Psalm 119:105).

Is every word of the Bible literally true, even when scientific data appears to contradict what it says?

This is an obviously important question for believers who believe the Bible to be the most important authority for the way they think and act as Christians. It is difficult to see how the Bible can exercise its authority if it is not true. However, the real question is *what kind of truth* does the Bible claim for itself? This is a topic on which there is ongoing Evangelical discussion, with most Evangelicals occupying one or the other of two positions. Those who affirm "infallibility" argue that the Bible's truth is limited to matters of faith and practice: the Bible tells us not how the heavens go but how to go to heaven. On this view, the Bible is a reliable guide to evangelism and theology, but not astronomy and biology. By contrast, Evangelicals who affirm "inerrancy" hold that God's word is a reliable guide on all matters that it addresses, though just what it *is* affirming remains a burning interpretive question. To what extent does the Bible make historical and scientific affirmations?

Critics and commentators only confuse matters when they suggest that inerrantists believe in the literal truth of every word of the Bible. In the first place, individual words are neither true nor false. That's because they do not *assert* anything. To assert something—to make a truth claim—is something people do by using words, but there are many other things we use words to do besides stating facts. Secondly, critics of inerrancy typically confuse "literal" with "literalistic" truth. Defenders of inerrancy must take great care to distinguish the notion of literal truth from the kind of literalistic interpretation that runs roughshod over the intent of the author and the literary form of the text. We'll return to this point in a moment.

The real issue, however, has to do with reliability (and here inerrantists and infallibilists agree): is the Bible a trustworthy guide? Does it lead us along the grain of reality, along the way of salvation? What is at stake in the doctrine of Scripture is our ability to trust that God is always a reliable speech agent, a promise-keeper and truth-teller rather than a liar or deceiver (see Numbers 23:19). The truthfulness of Scripture is ultimately tied to the trustworthiness of its manifold testimony to Jesus Christ. To say that Scripture is reliable is to say that it is not mistaken in what it intends to say and do. To say that it is infallible is to say that despite minor errors of history and science it will not fail to accomplish its purpose of presenting Christ and training in righteousness (2 Timothy 3:16). To say that Scripture is inerrant is to say that *God speaks through the human authors in Scripture truly, in all things it affirms, when it is rightly interpreted.* In order to understand the inerrantist tradition, we need to examine each element of this definition, including its final qualification.

We have already discussed how God speaks through the human authors of Scripture. We begin, then, with *truly.* To speak truly is to say of what is that it is (and of what is not that it is not). The ultimate truth that the Bible speaks is the truth about the one who is himself the truth, even Jesus Christ (John 14:6). As Luther says, the Bible presents (and represents) Christ. As the truth, Christ himself is a faithful representation of God, "the exact imprint of his nature" (Hebrews 1:3 ESV; compare John 14:9 ESV "whoever has seen me has seen the Father"). The truth of words is their reliable witness to reality, especially to *what is* "in Christ."

In all things it affirms. It is not words or texts that affirm things but authors, by means of words and texts. One must therefore do more than look up the definitions of individual words; one must ask what authors are doing with their words. For example, is everything an author says an affirmation? No, of course not: authors not only affirm but question things. Other things that authors *do* with words—"speech acts" like promising, warning, commanding and exhorting—are not affirmations either, though they may depend upon or presuppose affirmations (that is, beliefs about a certain state of affairs). The point is that not every sentence is a statement. We need to discern what the author is really *doing* with his words as opposed to what he appears to be saying. For example, is the author of Genesis 1–2 intending to teach the theory of the Big Bang, or a six-day creation, or something else? Was Jesus *affirming botanic truth* when he called the mustard seed "the smallest of all the seeds" (Mark 4:31 ESV), or was he *drawing an analogy* that his hearers would have understood in order to communicate a spiritual truth?

When it is rightly interpreted. Other notions may die the death of a thousand qualifications, but this single qualification is vital to the concept of inerrancy. To rightly interpret Scripture means recognizing what *kinds* of things the biblical authors are doing with their words. One way to do this is to determine a text's literary genre. Are we reading history, fiction, apocalyptic literature, wisdom, scientific instruction or something else? Is the author speaking figuratively or ironically? The question of meaning precedes the question of truth. One must first understand what an author has said before one can bring his text to judgment (that is, before one can decide whether it is true or false). Furthermore, we have to recognize that some of the Bible's genres are quite different from what we encounter in today's newspapers. The literary conventions of apocalyptic literature are not those of modern historiography. This does not mean that one is truer than the other, by the way, only that we need to recognize the conventions of each in order rightly to interpret what is being said. The above unpacking of the meaning of inerrancy allows us to resolve many, if not most, of the apparent contradictions between science and Scripture. Here are a few additional points to keep in mind, starting with some advice from Augustine: "And if in these writings I am perplexed by anything which appears to me opposed to truth, I do not hesitate to suppose that either the manuscript is faulty, or the translator has not caught the meaning of what was said, or I myself have failed to understand."[5] The last possibility is especially relevant: humility, both on the part of the scientist and the biblical interpreter, will go a long way in forestalling the premature objection that the "assured" results of science contradict Scripture.

Next, it is helpful to remember the distinction between adequacy and absoluteness. In debates over inerrancy, much depends on what one considers an error. Have I made an error if I say my manuscript is 80,000 words long when the total word count is 79,874? It all depends on one's expectation and on the context of my claim. In everyday conversation, round figures are perfectly acceptable; no one would accuse me of lying or deceiving. In other contexts, however, a different level of precision is required. My editor at Cambridge University Press, for example, may not take kindly to my smuggling in an extra 126 words (especially if she is paid by the word!). Here is my point: what counts as an error depends upon the kind of precision or exactness that the reader has a right to expect. "Error" is thus a context-dependent notion.

The question, then, is whether the Bible leads its readers to expect scientific exactness or absolute thoroughness. I think not. Too much precision is not only distracting but can actually hinder clear communication ("too much information!" we cry). If "error" is the failure to make good on one's claims, then the Bible's inerrancy means that its truth claims never fail to accomplish the particular communicative purpose for which they are sent.

Finally, how does inerrancy handle cases where God seems to adopt the limited perspective of human beings? For example, does the Bible assert that the sun "rises" every twenty-four hours when we know, from science, that it is the earth turning that creates that impression? The inerrantist here appeals to the notion of accommodation, which means that God adapts his speech to human conventions so that humans can

The Chicago Statement on Biblical Inerrancy. The Chicago Statement on Biblical Inerrancy was the outcome of a conference sponsored by the International Council on Biblical Inerrancy that met in Chicago in October 1978. Some two hundred Evangelical leaders, including Carl F. H. Henry, J. I. Packer, Francis Schaeffer and Robert Preus, agreed on a statement intended to stop the liberal drift away from affirming the Bible's truth in matters of history and science as well as faith and theology. The statement itself begins with five brief affirmations on Scripture's divine origin and verbal inspiration, followed by nineteen articles, each with an affirmation and denial (for example, Article VIII affirms that God uses "the distinctive personalities and literary styles" of the human authors and denies that God overrides their personalities in causing them to use the very words God chose). The Chicago Statement has become the authoritative touchstone for many, but not all, evangelical institutions. For example, the Evangelical Theological Society requires its members to affirm inerrancy. The document may be found online at bible-researcher.com/chicago1.html.[6]

understand him. To speak of the sun rising is to employ a social con-
vention, a way of speaking about natural phenomena that is true to our
everyday experience of the world. Divine accommodation serves the
purpose of divine communication, for in the final analysis, the Bible is
not a scientific textbook but a book of the covenant, a wholly reliable
account of what God was doing, in Christ, to reconcile the world to
himself (2 Corinthians 5:19).

3

WHO IS GOD?

George Kalantzis

Often, at thfe very heart of the question, *Who is God?*, lies our desire to know *if* there is a God; and *if* there is a God, how do we come to know this divine being, so removed and foreign to our own experiences?

My first training was as a natural scientist, a biologist, not as a theologian. As a college student, and then again as a graduate student in the natural sciences, I was trained to ask questions. I remember vividly looking up into the night sky and asking, "Is there anyone there?" How do I know? And *if* there is someone there, is it simply a "creative force," a "cosmic spirituality," to which we each come from our own vantage point and understanding? And how are we to receive all the competing claims about gods, and God, that so many religions make? How do we reach up and find out who God is?

We, of course, are neither the first nor the only ones to ask such questions. From Job to Abraham to Thomas, and even Pontius Pilate himself, the Bible is full of the stories of people who ask questions very similar to ours.

The first time someone records one's own, first person, account with God in the Bible is found in the book of Exodus. In Exodus 3, Moses records his own encounter with God at the place of the "burning bush," and the questions he asks are exactly our own questions: *Who is God? How do we know which one is the true God? Whom do we trust?*

To understand what happened in this encounter, however, we have to remember who Moses was. Moses was born to Hebrew parents from the tribe of Levi when the Israelites were still in Egypt. While still a baby, Moses was adopted by one of Pharaoh's daughters who raised him as her own in the palace (Exodus 2:1-10; Acts 7:20-21). Unlike the DreamWorks version, *The Prince of Egypt*, he was not a rebelling teenager when he encountered one of his fellow Egyptians abusing one of his Hebrew kin. Moses was a mature man of forty years at the time (Acts 7:23). He had been educated "in all the wisdom of the Egyptians," and was "powerful in speech and action" (Acts 7:22). As a member of Pharaoh's household, educated in the best schools of his time, Moses was also steeped in the religious life and culture of the Egyptians—that is a large part of what "the wisdom of the Egyptians" means. Moses knew very well the character and cosmic power of the gods of Egypt, of Ra, and Nut, of Osiris, of Amun, of Isis and Heh. Moses understood the divine right of kings and the immense power carried by their very names.

During that fateful event, when he came to the defense of the abused Hebrew slave, Moses killed an Egyptian and, as a result, had to flee from Egypt (Exodus 2:11-15). Moses found refuge among the Midianites, where he settled, marrying Zipporah, a daughter of the priest Jethro, "the priest of Midian" (Exodus 3:1). Moses lived among the Midianites for another forty years, learning their ways, worshiping their gods, settling in among them and raising a family (Acts 7:29; Exodus 2:16-22).

In the first forty years of his life, Moses had become an expert in the religion of the Egyptians. He had asked the questions with which we began, *Who is God?*, and had been given answers that placed the Egyptian gods at the center. During the next forty years of his life, Moses engaged the religion of the Midianites, and the answers he received were different. And now, at the age of eighty, while tending the flock of his father-in-law, Moses came to investigate the marvelous sign he saw: a bush that was aflame but was not consumed (Exodus 3:2).

It is here, at Horeb, on the "far side of the wilderness," in sight of the "burning bush," that we have the first, first-person account of God speaking. God called out to Moses with these words: "I am the God of your father, the God of Abraham, the God of Isaac and the God of Jacob" (Exodus 3:6). Moses reacted the only way a person would: "Moses hid his face, because he was afraid to look at God" (Exodus 3:6). We know the rest of the story. God was about to give Moses a mission he never expected. He was to return to Egypt and lead God's people out of Egypt

(Exodus 3:10). Sometimes, however, we miss what happened next: Moses hesitated. How could a fugitive, eighty-year-old nomad stand up to Pharaoh, the most powerful ruler of his time?

Now, it is at this part of the story where all the questions we asked before come together. You see, when Moses received God's promise that this was not his mission to accomplish by himself, but that God would be with him (Exodus 3:12), Moses turned to God and asked: "Suppose I go to the Israelites and say to them, 'The God of your fathers has sent me to you,' and they ask me, 'What is his name?' Then what shall I tell them?" (Exodus 3:13). Moses is asking of God: *What is [your] name?* If we stop here and ponder what Moses is asking we realize that Moses was *not* asking, *What do I call you?* No, what Moses was asking God was, *Who are you? How do I know you are true? How can I trust you?*

God's response to Moses' question is "I AM WHO I AM" (Exodus 3:14). God's self-identification as "I AM" destroyed everything Moses thought he knew about the divine reality and confounded his categories. Why? Because like most of us, Moses' expectations for who God is began with the experiences of the world that surrounds us and assumed that the same could apply to God. We engage and experience each other and the world around us through our perception of categories of being, of nouns. Trees may vary in height and fruit, in shape and in color, but at the end, they all belong to the same class of being: they are all trees. The same holds true of humans. Though we may differ in gender, age, ethnicity, height, accent, color or social location, all human beings belong to the same class of being. We make sense of the world as we recognize things and ourselves by comparing one thing to another and by identifying the relationships that govern them. That is exactly how Moses approached the question of who God is. Like us, Moses was asking God, *From among the category of beings called "god," which one are you?* and, *Are you more powerful than the gods of Egypt? Does your name carry the awesome authority of Ra, the sun-god?*

God's self-identification as "I AM" is a claim of uniqueness of existence, at once declaring all other "deities" not as lesser, or inadequate, but simply as nonexistent. In this exchange with Moses, God showed us that the word *God* does not refer to a noun, a category or a class of beings that share in the properties of the noun, whether those properties relate to knowledge, power or even time, or share in the "essence" of *God*. Nor is the I AM an additional element in Moses' lifetime of religious education; the imaginatively complex systems Moses had learned and used to explain the universe are shattered. God repeats this again and again in Scripture, even in the time of Isaiah, centuries later, when God declares: "I am the LORD, and there is no other" (Isaiah 45:18).

God's self-identification as "I AM," then, sets God apart from all other manner of existence. "God" is not a noun, indicative of a class or category of beings that share in particular characteristics. Rather, "God" is the very *name* of the I AM. To our basic questions, then, *Is there a God?* and if so, *Which one of the many in our religious systems is the true God?* God responds with a very clear: "I AM, and there is no other!"

If God is not part of our experience, isn't all talk about God just a guessing game?

The Bible is quite clear from the very beginning that the only reason we can *know* God or speak *of* God is because God *spoke first*, revealing God's self to us. Theologian Joe R. Jones reminds us that "the most commanding image of God in the Old Testament is *God speaking*: God speaking to persons, God commanding persons, instructing persons."[1] It was God's own self-revelation that allowed Moses to begin to understand who God is, and how to think and speak of God. We understand, therefore, that we can speak of God not because the rest of our experiences have prepared us to do so, but simply because God spoke to us first.

In its most basic form, *theology* is the task of *speaking about God*.[2] From our own, everyday language we realize that in order to understand each other we need to accept and use rules of grammar and syntax that give meaning to our words and help us communicate. Our speech about God is no different in this regard. To make sense of what we say about God, we need to agree upon and use what we could term the essential "grammar of Christian faith" so that our *theology*, our speech about God, may be properly understood.

One of the most basic principles of this grammar of Christian faith is that when we speak of God, we do not attempt to *define* who God is, but simply *describe* how God has revealed God's own self to us from the beginning. Another principle is that God is not an *object* to be studied. When we analyze and study an object, whether that is an idea, a molecule or a star, we stand over and above that object and we decide what that object *is* and what it *can* and *cannot* be. In other words, we have authority over the object of our study. This is not true with God. We do not discover or analyze God; God speaks to us. It is God who has the authority to tell us what is true and what is not. Therefore, third, God is the *agent* who reveals, not the *object* who is studied. God *personally* creates, acts in history, and reveals God's self to us. This, fourth, means that God is a *free* subject. Neither creation nor this self-revelation is necessary for God to be God. Finally, God's self-revelation is *true* revelation of God's self. Because God is the agent, we can safely trust our limited words to be fitting descriptions of who God is and how God acts in history (compare Numbers 23:19; Titus 1:2).

Everything we can say about God is, at the end, derivative, a reflection back to the source of the self-revelation we try to describe. As God commanded Moses: "This is what you are to say . . . " (Exodus 3:14).

Is the God of the Old Testament different from the God of the New Testament?

The simple answer to this question is "No." Christians believe that from the first chapter of the book of Genesis to the last chapter of the book of Revelation it is the same God who reveals God's self throughout the Bible. In the epistle to the Hebrews the author begins the letter by answering the same question: "In the past God spoke to our ancestors through the prophets at many times and in various ways, but in these last days he has spoken to us by his Son" (Hebrews 1:1-2). However, even though Jesus came into the history of the world almost 400 years after the last book of the Old Testament was written, Christians believe that since he is God the Son, God incarnate, the second person of the divine Trinity, Jesus is the self-revelation of God. As such, our understanding of who God is has to begin with Jesus. He provides the filter through which Christians understand not only the New Testament, but also the Old. Properly speaking, then, Christian theology begins with the person of Jesus Christ.

To use John's language: Jesus is "the Word [who] became flesh and made his dwelling among us" (John 1:14). The life, death and resurrection of Jesus of Nazareth establishes a new "vocabulary of divinity" in a manner not seen before.

> The *self-revelation* of God finds its normative and definitive expression in the life, death and resurrection of Jesus of Nazareth. It is his story that gives the language of theology its context.

As we will see in the chapters, "Who Is Jesus?" and "Who is the Holy Spirit?", because the Word, the Son, is one of the three Persons of the divine Trinity, the self-revelation of God in the person of Jesus Christ through the Holy Spirit (compare John 16:12; 1 Corinthians 12:3; 1 John 5:7 and so on) reveals to us the very character of God, and allows us to "*speak of God.*" The Bible tells us that Jesus is indeed God incarnate (John 1:1, 14), in whom "the whole fullness of deity dwells bodily" (Colossians 2:9 ESV). God's *self-revelation* in Jesus transforms our understanding. From the earliest times, Christians have affirmed that the Incarnation provides the lens through which we are to understand the world, history and even language itself.

What is this "vocabulary of divinity" all about?

From the earliest years, Christians recognized that since God does not belong to our customary categories of experience, we cannot describe

> The fact that God's revelation in Jesus Christ is self-revelation *also* means that even though one cannot comprehend the substance or nature of God, the words spoken about God are not meaningless. They truly *describe*, though they do not *define*, God.

who God is in God's self or essence in the same way we describe how God relates to the world and the created order. Even though we recognize that our ability to describe who God is in God's own self is very limited, God has given to us in Scripture a language to describe the essential reality and oneness of God (think of Deuteronomy 6:4-9). In theology, we call this the *immanent Trinity*. When we describe how God acts beyond the triune self we use language that has come to us from the early Church. The earliest Christians used the language of *economy*, drawing an analogy from the management of the affairs of a household

The Nicene Creed

We believe in one God, Father almighty, maker of heaven and earth, of all things visible and invisible;

And in one Lord Jesus Christ, the only begotten Son of God, begotten from the Father before all ages, Light from Light, true God of true God, begotten not made, of one essence with the Father, through whom all things came into existence, who because of us human beings and because of our salvation came down from the heavens, and was incarnate from the Holy Spirit and the Virgin Mary, and became man, and was crucified under Pontius Pilate, and suffered and was buried, and rose again on the third day according to the Scriptures and ascended into heaven, and sits on the right hand of the Father, and will come again with glory to judge the living and the dead, of whose kingdom there will be no end.

And in the Holy Spirit, the Lord and Giver of Life, who proceeds from the Father, who with the Father and Son is together worshipped and together glorified, who spoke through the prophets; In one, holy, catholic, and apostolic Church. We confess one baptism for the remission of sins; We look forward to the resurrection of the dead and the life of the world to come. Amen.

to describe the triune God's active plan and management of the world and its history. In this case, we speak of the *economic Trinity.*

The historic Creeds of the Church (such as the Apostles' Creed, or the Nicene Creed) provide the structure within which Christians can express our faith and make sense of the self-revelation of God. Why is this structure necessary? When Moses saw the burning bush, nothing in the "grammar" of his eighty years of experiences had prepared him for the new "vocabulary" of the self-revelation of God, but in God's presence he took off his shoes and listened. The ordinary had been transformed. In the same way, the historic Creeds of the Church structure our own experiences on how to understand the God who is revealed to us in Scripture. Like Moses, nothing in our own experience, either, has prepared us to understand that this God whom Moses met for the first time at Horeb, is triune: Father, Son and Holy Spirit.

The Trinity sounds like nonsense to me. What does it mean? And why does it matter?

If you have managed to come to this point of our discussion you have undoubtedly noticed that I have avoided using the first person singular masculine pronoun "him/his" to refer to God. The reason for that is not that I don't like gender-specific language (we will deal with the question "Is God male?" later), but because either singular or plural pronouns could be misunderstood. In *our* time, with *our* use of language and *our* habits of understanding, one could read the pronoun "he/his" and assume God to be a singularity. So, in order to avoid this confusion, I have used "God" and "God's self" instead.

That God is Father, Son and Holy Spirit is the witness of the whole of Scriptures, both the Old and the New Testaments, and as we will see in the chapters "Who Is Jesus?" and "Who Is the Holy Spirit?", the Bible is consistent in speaking of the Father as God, of the Son as God and of the Holy Spirit as God. The confession of God as triune is based on God's own revelation of God's own self to God's people, and it is, therefore, a foundational confession for Christians. In everything we say about God we have to maintain a delicate balance between both *real oneness* and *real distinction* at once, because that is also how Scripture speaks of God.

Throughout its history, the Church recognized at least three major problems with language that create for us a concept of God that is neither true nor biblical. The first one is the danger of *tritheism.* Tritheism is a simplified form of the polytheism that was so prevalent in the ancient world. Tritheism argues that Father, Son and Holy Spirit are three gods, like Zeus, Mars and Poseidon were three gods for the Greeks and the Romans. Jews and Christians utterly rejected this *classical* form of tritheism based on the very declaration of God: "Hear, O Israel, the LORD our God, the LORD is one" (Deuteronomy 6:4) and the prohibition found in the first Commandment (Exodus 20:3). The very first clause of the historic creed of the church begins with this declaration: "We believe in one God, Father almighty, maker of heaven and earth, of all things visible and invisible."

Yet, Christians can tend toward a less obvious form of tritheism that is equally as dangerous and as rejected by the Church. This *incipient tritheism* maintains that even though the Father, the Son and the Holy Spirit share the same common essence, they are three separate, distinct subjects or agents, each with a *distinct mind* and *will* coming together in one divine activity. This form of tritheism holds that the trinity is a unity of three wills and operations, much like three human voices coming together to produce a *harmony* out of a single note. This form of tritheism sees the Trinity as one essence with three *instances*, coming together in perfect unity to be one God. While attractive and providing an answer to the *real distinction* in the Trinity, this form of tritheism loses the *real oneness* of God. From the earliest years of the Church, Christians understood that there cannot be three distinct centers of attribution, consciousness, and operation, or three distinct wills in God—that is, God is not three individuals capable of separately saying "I will," or "I AM." The analogy of the harmony sung by three voices may apply to human beings, but it is not true of the triune God. In the late fourth century, Gregory of Nyssa, one of the most influential theologians of the Church, saw the danger and used the example of three distinct people, Peter, James and Paul to explain the difference. Here is what he said:

> Among people, because the activity of each is distinguished, although in
> the same pursuit [for example singing a single note], they are properly

mentioned in the plural. . . . But in reference to divine nature, we have learned that this is not the case, as if the Father does something individually, in which the Son does not join, or the Son individually works something without the Spirit. Rather, every activity that comes from God to creation, whatever that activity may be, starts off from the Father, proceeds through the Son, and is completed by the Holy Spirit. On account of this the name of activity is not divided into the multitude of those who are active.[3]

Because God, Father, Son and Holy Spirit, is *truly one*, there is one *will*, one *mind* and *one* operation in God. Yet, there is also *real distinction* in the Trinity, but that is not a distinction of will or of essence—it is a distinction of how the *one* will of God is brought into effect.

Incipient tritheism is dangerous because it sounds biblical and it uses Christian language, but it locates God's oneness in a combination analogous to human beings. This type of personhood may be attractive to modern ideas of "individualism" and "personalism," but it does not apply to the triune God. One cannot apply the same concept of "person" we use to understand people to the divine "persons," Father, Son and Holy Spirit.

On the other side of the spectrum, the second danger is *modalism*. Modalism obliterates any distinction between Father, Son and Holy Spirit. While historically diverse, *modalism* thinks of God as a singularity, a monadic God who appeared in history sometimes under the name (or *mode*) of "Father," other times as "Son," and yet other times under the name "Holy Spirit." Modalism sees God like an actor who plays three distinct characters, rejecting any real distinction between Father, Son and Holy Spirit. For instance, one form of modalism is called *Patripassianism* (which means, *"the Father suffers"*). This form of modalism argues that because the Father and the Son are not truly different, the incarnation was the incarnation of the Father, who suffered and died on the cross. Because modalism denies any *real distinction* in God, it cannot interpret the many instances in the New Testament where Jesus prayed to the Father (for example, John 17) as anything other than hollow words without true meaning. At worst, God's revelation as triune becomes a cosmic farce.

The third danger is that of *subordinationism*. Subordinationism tries to protect the *real distinction* in God by denying the deity of the Son and the Spirit. Subordinationism claims that the one, true God is the Father, and that the Son and the Spirit were created by God. Sometimes the Son is seen as the very first and most brilliant of God's creatures (this is how Jehovah's Witnesses read, for example, Colossians 1:15 ESV, where the Son is described as the "firstborn of all creation"), while other times Jesus is seen simply as the natural son of Joseph and Mary "adopted" by the Father during his baptism (for example, Matthew 3:17) because he was obedient to the will of the Father.

Because Jesus became human and was obedient to the Father during the incarnation (for example, John 5:19-24; 14:28), this movement sees this as an eternal subordination in the Trinity. It may affirm the life, suffering and death of Jesus, but among the many problems with this form of subordinationism, the church historically sees this as an issue of salvation. In the end, if Son and Spirit are not true God, they are not "God" at all. Christians confess Jesus as the savior of the world and God's own self-revelation.

That's why it matters very much that we learn to speak of the triune God properly. Because, if Jesus is not God, God is not our savior (as Isaiah 43:11 would suggest) and our salvation was effected by the death of a creature.

How do the Father, Son and Holy Spirit relate to each other? Isn't the Father more important than Jesus and the Spirit?

Karl Barth was one of the great theologians of the twentieth century. When he described how Christians ought to speak of God he said that "The one name of God is the threefold name of Father, Son, and Holy Spirit . . . the one 'personality' of God, the one active and speaking *Ego* is Father, Son, and Holy Spirit. Otherwise we should obviously have to speak of three gods."[4]

When we speak of God, we have to maintain a delicate balance between both *real oneness* and *real distinction* at once. To understand more fully the *real oneness* of God, we have to recognize that God is not composed of various parts; God is *simple*. As we saw earlier, we also need to keep in mind that Father, Son and Spirit are not three individual personalities, wills or beings, coming together to form a unity or harmony. Rather, the Father, Son and Spirit are in what theologians term "*consubstantial* relationship of mutual *interexistence*." This is a way of saying that what is *one* in God is God's *essence*.

Christians have learned through much trial and error in our attempts to find what language best describes the triune God. However, since we cannot *define* God, but can only *describe* God, we cannot *define* the "essence" of God, either. To ask the question: "What is the essence of God— or, what is God made of?" is nonsensical. We always have to keep in mind that God is not a category of things nor does God have essence we can examine, dissect, or catalog. When Christians say that God the Father, God the Son and God the Holy Spirit are *of one essence*, we do not try to respond to the question "What is the essence of God?" The statement simply states the fact of the relationship.

If what is one in God is *essence*, the word we use to describe what is three in God is *person*. So, when we speak of God, we speak of one *essence* in three *persons*. This back-and-forth between language of *real oneness* and language of *real difference* is also how the Scriptures speak of God from Genesis to Revelation.

It is quite easy for us to utter the words and say: "We, Christians, confess God as Trinity," but to describe what that means is not that simple! Even the famous theologian of the early Church, Gregory of Nazianzus, had to admit to this: "No sooner do I consider the One than I am enlightened by the radiance of the Three; no sooner do I distinguish them than I am carried back to the One."[5] If we stop our description of who God is at the statement that Father, Son and Spirit are of *one essence*, we run the danger of being led to modalism. That is why we need to speak of the *real difference* almost in the same breath as we speak of *real oneness*. To describe the *real difference*, Christians look to how God acts in history and recognize that there are particular actions of God that are *appropriate to* (or *appropriated by*) a specific Person of the Trinity. For example, it was the Son, the second person of the Trinity, who was nailed on the cross, not the Father (Matthew 27). It was the Holy Spirit who breathed (new) life into the disciples and filled them (Acts 2), not the Son. It was the Father who said, "Let us create" (Genesis 1:26) and who sent the "only begotten Son" (John 3:16 KJV). Yet, the Scriptures reveal that every action of God is inseparably triune. Every action of God is, at the same time, an action of Father, Son and Spirit.

Among the manifold witness of Scripture we hear Jesus' own statements that "The Son can do nothing by himself; he can do only what he sees his Father doing, because whatever the Father does the Son also does" (John 5:19, and so on). The triune persons act inseparably, albeit in an ordered manner. Here is how another early Christian theologian, Gregory of Nyssa, explained it:

> The principle of the power of oversight and beholding in Father, Son, and Holy Spirit is one. It starts off from the Father as from a spring; it is effected by the Son, and by the power of the Spirit it completes its grace. No activity is divided to the *Persons*, completed individually by each and set apart without being viewed together. . . . All providence, care, and attention of all, both of things in sensible creation and things of the heavenly nature . . . is one and not three, kept straight by the Holy Trinity.[6]

This is *not* a hierarchy of essence, or of will, or of status. This is an ordered working out of God's actions in the history of the cosmos. Every action of God is a triune action. But when we look at how God interacts with the world, there are two questions that go hand-in-hand. The first is a question of "Who?" while the second a question of "How?"

When we ask the question, "*Who* created the world?" Scripture's simple answer is that it was the one God (Father, Son and Holy Spirit) who did. When we ask, "*How* did God create?" the Scriptures tell us that creation originates from the Father (Genesis 1:1), it comes to be through the agency of the Son (John 1:1-2; Colossians 1:16-17), and it is brought to completion by the Holy Spirit (Genesis 1:2). The same is true for every other action of God. Look, for example, at the work of salvation: it begins with the Father (John 3:16), it is effected by and through the incarnation of the Son (John 1:14; 3:16), and it is made possible by the power of the Spirit (Luke 1:35). In Romans 8:11 Paul makes this clear, speaking about the resurrection of our bodies: "And if the Spirit of him [that is, Father] who raised Jesus from the dead is living in you, he [that is, Father] who raised Christ from the dead will also give life to your mortal bodies because of his Spirit who lives in you." The Father raised the Son through the power and agency of the Holy Spirit.

These two descriptions, then, of the *real oneness*, on the one hand, and of the *real difference*, on the other, always have to be *thought of* and be *spoken of* together—almost in unison. For they provide the basic rule of the "grammar of divinity" for Christian speech about God.

Why do we say, "We believe in one God, the Father"? Is God male?

This is a very serious question with real life implications for our common life together. Language gives expression to our thoughts and emotions; it gives meaning to our experiences. The language we use not only forms us into who we are, it also shapes our understanding of the world and everything in it.

Many of us come from broken families. Some of us have had such traumatic experiences with our own parents that it is almost impossible for us to address God as Father—for every time we do so, we experience anew the abuse, abandonment, and fear we associate with the name. Worse yet, throughout the history of the Church, even today, many men have attempted to hide their thirst for power and control with appeals to the "fatherhood" of God. If God is male, the argument goes, then men ought to be the ones in positions of power. The witness of Scripture to any such attempt to misuse the name of God is an unequivocal "No! God is not male."

From the earliest expressions of the Church, Christians understood that how we use language in worship forms how we understand God and ourselves. They even had a short phrase to describe that: *lex orandi, lex credendi*, loosely translatable as "*the law (or language) of prayer is the law (or language) of belief.*" The relationship between worship, faith and life is an unbreakable one. At the end, it is *in* our prayer and worship that we truly learn *what* we believe and *how* to live our lives. The language of our prayer and worship forms our system of faith and forces us to see God and ourselves in that particular way, the way in which our language leads us to.

That is why we began with a discussion on how to speak of God properly. Throughout our discussion we have seen that the witness of Scripture is consistent: God is *simple* (that is, not composed of parts), *immutable, impassible, infinite,* and that essence and existence are identical in God. It ought to be clear, then, that God does not have a genotype whose phenotypical expression would indicate maleness, like it does for us. Since God is not part of a category, it follows that God *cannot* be part of the category designated by the noun "male."

Yet, Scripture speaks of God using the first person masculine pronoun "He." What are we to do with that? How are we to reconcile the fact that even though God is *not* a gendered being, *how* we speak of God frames our understanding both of God and of ourselves? How can we avoid extolling "maleness" and elevating one-half of humanity in a position of authority and power over the other half? What we have to do is to keep always in mind that evil rarely manifests itself apocalyptically; rather, it creeps into our lives and society. Mary Daly so provocatively noted the incipient nature of this danger when she exclaimed: "If God is male, then the male is God."[7]

Even in the fourth century, Gregory of Nazianzus recognized this danger and spoke of the role and importance of language in shaping our very understanding of who God is. He wrote: "Some of you would consider our God to be male, . . . because he is called *Theos* [(the word 'God' is masculine in Greek)] and Father, and that *Theiotis* [(Deity)] is feminine, from the gender of the word, and Spirit neuter, because 'It' has nothing to do with generation." That, Gregory concludes, is "just silly."[8]

What Gregory is telling us is that if we keep firmly in our mind that "God" is not a noun but a *name,* then we also realize that for the triune God of the Scriptures, "Father," "Son" and "Holy Spirit" are not nouns either—they are proper names. The Son addresses the Father as "Father" (John 17:1) not because there is a relationship of generation between Father and Son, but simply because this is the proper name of the first person of the Trinity. And the Father does not address the Son as "Son" (Mark 1:11) because the Father gave birth to the Son, but because that is the proper name of the second person of the Trinity. The same holds true for the third person, whose proper name is "Spirit." Here is how Basil of Caesarea puts it: "When the Lord taught us the doctrine of Father, Son,

So, who is God? The true objects of enjoyment are the Father and the Son and the Holy Spirit, who are at the same time the Trinity, one being, supreme above all, and common to all who enjoy him, if God is an object, and not rather the cause of all objects, or indeed even if God is the cause of all.

It is not easy to find a name that will suitably express so great an excellence, unless it is better to speak in this way: the Trinity, one God, *of whom* are all things, *through whom* are all things, *in whom* are all things.

Thus the Father and the Son and the Holy Spirit, and each of these by himself, is God, and at the same time they are all one God; and each of them by himself is a complete substance, and yet they are all one substance.

The Father is not the Son nor the Holy Spirit; the Son is not the Father nor the Holy Spirit; the Holy Spirit is not the Father nor the Son: but the Father is only Father, the Son is only Son, and the Holy Spirit is only Holy Spirit.

To all three belong the same eternity, the same unchangeableness, the same majesty, the same power. In the Father is unity, in the Son equality, in the Holy Spirit the harmony of unity and equality.

And these three attributes are all one because of the Father, all equal because of the Son, and all harmonious because of the Holy Spirit.[11]

and Holy Spirit, . . . He blessed us with the knowledge given us by faith, by means of holy Names."[9] In other words: The one name of the one God is the threefold *name* of Father, Son and Holy Spirit. So, why do we address the Father as "Father"? Because Jesus did (John 17:1). Because this is the name of the first Person of the Trinity—and for no other reason.

So, then, how are we to understand God as Father?

I have found no better—short—answer than that given by Garrett

Green in his essay, *The Gender of God and the Theology of Metaphor*. Green speaks of a subtle distinction between *understanding* God as male and *speaking* of God.

> God is not male, yet the appropriate language in which to describe, address, and worship him is nevertheless masculine. Such masculinity is one grammatical aspect of the paradigmatic biblical narrative through which he has disclosed himself to Israel and the church. Read in context, however, this masculinity turns out to be "kenotic," an aspect of the divine self-emptying [Phil 2:7] by which God divests himself of all majesty, dominion, and power in order to overcome the powers (masculine and otherwise) of this word. Those whose imaginations are captured by this story will continue to receive it, in all its scandalous particularity, as the gift of God. For it enables them to do what would otherwise be impossible: to know, to love, and to praise the one true God, Father, Son, and Holy Spirit—and that can only mean in culturally particular—language.[10]

4

HOW DOES GOD RELATE
TO THE WORLD?

Gregory W. Lee

Few questions are more critical to Christian life and thought than how God relates to the world. At the deepest level, understanding the distinction between Creator and creation humbles us and fills us with awe. David expresses his wonder like this: "When I consider your heavens, the work of your fingers, the moon and the stars, which you have set in place, what are mere mortals that you are mindful of them, human beings that you care for them?" (Psalm 8:3-4 TNIV).

A more controversial issue has to do with science. Confessing a God who works actively in the world can be tricky because such beliefs are often associated with anti-intellectualism and a posture of suspicion toward modern discovery. I recall attending my ten-year high school reunion when I had completed a master's degree from seminary and recently begun a doctoral program in theology. The first question my old classmates would ask me after they learned what I was doing was strikingly consistent: "Why are Christians so against science? How can they not believe in evolution?"

Beyond these complex debates, Christians of all stripes wonder about God's plan for their lives, how to discern God's will and whether God really hears prayer. We cannot experience the freedom and assurance of the Christian life without some belief in God's sovereignty over all things.

There are many disagreements between Christians on the details of God's activity in the world—in part because such questions involve mysteries beyond our understanding—but there are some broad affirmations that Christians have shared throughout the history of the church.

First, God created the world. This assertion is found in the first verse of the Bible, and the opening remarks of John's Gospel. "In the beginning God created the heavens and the earth" (Genesis 1:1). "Through [the Word] all things were made; without him nothing was made that has been made" (John 1:3). Theologians have long held that God created the world from nothing (ex nihilo). There literally was "no thing" that existed before God made it because all things derive their being from him. This means, among other implications, that God stands utterly distinct from and transcendent over the world.

Second, God continues to work actively in the world. God did not simply wind up the world like a clock, then let the gears start turning according to the laws of nature. According to Hebrews, the Son continues to sustain all things by his word (Hebrews 1:3). God's ongoing involvement with the world does not preclude the existence of scientific laws and principles; God uses consistent means to govern the universe. But there is a sense in which God is the ultimate source and cause of all that comes to be.

Third, God created humans as responsible agents who can participate in God's plans for the world. How exactly humans may be considered free if God governs history is one of the great questions of theology and philosophy, and other sections of this chapter and book will address this issue more fully. But the classic Christian position has been to affirm some kind of "both-and." It is true *both* that God is sovereign over the world *and* that humans may exercise free choice such that they can be held accountable for their actions.

Fourth, God has a glorious plan for the world. The story of redemption would not be much of a story if there were no promise of a blessed hope. This promise grounds our confidence that God is involved with the world now, shaping the course of human affairs according to his final ends. "And we know that in all things God works for the good of those who love him, who have been called according to his purpose" (Romans 8:28). Even in the midst of suffering and evil, when this is very difficult to believe, God remains the Lord of history and will bring his purposes for the world to completion.

Now, then, let us consider some of the complexities.

What was God doing before the creation of the world?

Some ancient writers had a ready answer to this question: God was preparing a place to punish the overly curious! I think a more serious response is deserved, for this question raises fundamental issues about the nature of God and how God relates to us.

The key point to note is that God transcends time. God is the Alpha and the Omega, the beginning and the end, the one who was and is and is to come. He is eternal (Revelation 1:8; 21:6; 22:13). Such a concept is impossible for humans to grasp fully because we are time-bound. We perceive the passing of moments such that the future becomes the present and the present becomes the past. But God does not experience the world this way. In a sense, God contains all time within himself, as if he perceived the past, present and future simultaneously. All times are equally present to him.

Philosophers and theologians have often identified the creation of time with the creation of the world. For them, that is, time began to exist when the universe began to exist. The reason for this position is that time is closely associated with motion (for how could we discern the passing of time if we did not observe movement?), and motion can only occur in physical things (since only physical things have bodies that move). Since God is spirit and does not have a body, he cannot move and does not exist in time.

In a technical sense, then, the original question of this section is grammatically incorrect. There is no "before the creation of the world" to speak of, for the very first moment of time coincides with the beginning of the world. God was not doing anything differently "before" creation, because there is no "before" or "during" or "after" for God. As Hebrews says of Jesus, God is the same "yesterday and today and forever" (Hebrews 13:8). The mysteries of God's timelessness are a reminder to us of the distinction between Creator and creation.

Could God create a rock so heavy he could not lift it?

Another paradoxical question! I remember when friends from youth group would ask this of retreat speakers as a practical joke to see how flustered these pastors would become. Yet again, this question bears upon more serious matters than might initially appear.

The issue at stake here is the character of God's omnipotence. Omnipotence is one of those "all" words we like to affirm about God: all-knowing, all-good, all-powerful. Does God's character as all-powerful mean he can do all things? The answer, somewhat counter intuitively, has to be no. There are countless things God cannot do. God cannot lie (Hebrews 6:18). God cannot be tempted by sin (James 1:13). God cannot violate his covenant or go back on his word (Romans 11:29). God cannot deny himself (2 Timothy 2:13; the apostle says this specifically of Christ, but we can apply the teaching to all the divine persons).

Suppose you had a kind grandmother who would wake you up from bed every morning, prepare you breakfast, pack your lunch and drive you to school. Then suppose someone reported to you that your grandmother had gone to the post office and shot all the employees and was now heading to the grocery store for more bloodshed. Your first reaction would probably be, "My grandmother could never do such a thing! You must be talking about the wrong person!" Such a statement would not be a judgment about whether your grandmother was physically strong enough to pick up a gun and pull the trigger. She could very well have that basic capacity. The focus of your response would rather be her moral character: "Given the kind of person I know my grandmother to be, she is incapable of such actions."

This is very similar to what theologians mean when they deny God can do all things. Qualifications about God's omnipotence are not meant to suggest that God is somehow weak or incapable of accomplishing his will. The God of creation can certainly do as he pleases (Jeremiah 32:17; Matthew 19:26; Ephesians 3:20). Any restrictions upon what God can do must therefore come from within. God is not constrained by external forces, but only by the consistency of his character and the quality of his desires. Would God ever want to lie, sin, go back on his word or deny himself? Of course not, and we do not reduce the power of God by rejecting the possibility.

We might, then, reframe the original question. The issue is not: *could* God create a rock so heavy he could not lift it? It is rather: *would* God create a rock so heavy he could not lift it? The answer, I think, is no. God would not produce such a situation because it would involve a denial of his power and authority over the world. And for this, we should give thanks.

Did God create the world in six days?

Many evangelicals believe so, but other evangelicals would take a different position. Such debate is not unusual. Throughout church history, important authors have recognized the difficulties surrounding the earliest chapters of Genesis.

One oft-cited example is Augustine, a fifth-century author and bishop, whose theology would exercise profound influence on western Christianity. In his commentary on Genesis, Augustine took the creation account of Genesis 2–3 quite literally: God really created Adam from dust; Adam really lived in a paradise with fruit trees; Adam and Eve really had a certain number of children and lived a certain number of years. But Augustine did not think the creation account of the preceding chapter, Genesis 1, demanded belief that God created the world in twenty-four-hour blocks of time. For Augustine, God created the world simultaneously, and the six days were a kind of literary device explaining the categories of creation. (Reminder: Augustine was writing over fourteen hundred years before Darwin.)

Perhaps the most valuable lesson we can receive from Augustine concerns his basic intellectual approach toward matters concerning faith and science. Augustine was frustrated by those in his day who insisted dogmatically on particular interpretations of difficult passages of Scripture when those texts concerned events far removed from our direct experience, and various interpretations could be accepted without undermining fundamental tenets of the faith. Augustine had no doubts about the authority of Scripture; he simply recognized that certain passages are very difficult to interpret and we may not always be able to determine the right meaning. He thus held his own position somewhat lightly and encouraged others to do the same.

As a text, Genesis 1 clearly reflects poetic elements, and the challenge for Christians is to discern how to understand them. On the one hand, the literary character of a text does not mean the text is simply mythological. Genesis 1 is making historical claims. On the other hand, the authority of Scripture does not demand reading every passage as a blow-by-blow account of historical events. We should at least pause before concluding definitively that the days must refer to literal twenty-four-hour periods of time.

Indeed, closer examination of Genesis 1 suggests alternate possibilities than straightforward historical description. In Genesis 1:2, the author writes that the earth was "formless" and "empty." The subsequent series of "days" yields a curious pattern.

Table 4.1

	"Formless"		"Empty"
Day 1	Light and darkness	Day 4	Sun, moon, stars
Day 2	Waters and sky	Day 5	Sea animals and birds
Day 3	Dry ground and vegetation	Day 6	Land animals and humans

Augustine on Genesis. In the beginning of the fifth century, Augustine presented this criticism of Christians who asserted dogmatic readings of Genesis with no real understanding of science. This quotation serves as an encouragement to humility in the interpretation of difficult passages.

It frequently happens that even non-Christians will have knowledge of [creation] in a way that they can substantiate with scientific arguments or experiments. Now it is quite disgraceful and disastrous, something to be on one's guard against at all costs, that they should ever hear Christians spouting what they claim our Christian literature has to say on these topics, and talking such nonsense that they can scarcely contain their laughter when they see them to be *toto caelo*, as the saying goes, wide of the mark. And what is so vexing is not that misguided people should be laughed at, as that our authors should be assumed by outsiders to have held such views, and to the great detriment of those about whose salvation we are so concerned, should be written off and consigned to the waste paper basket as so many ignoramuses.[1]

As this table shows, Days 1-3 correspond nicely to Days 4-6. On Days 1-3, God produces the "forms" or basic structures of the created order. On Days 4-6, God populates these structures with appropriate things, filling in what was formerly "empty." Modern readers are quick to point out that the sun, moon and stars were created on Day 4, though light and darkness were created on Day 1. (Christian writers at least as far back as the third century noted the same curiosity.) Our table suggests Day 4 should not be understood as chronologically posterior to Day 1. And this naturally makes one wonder whether these "Days" were intended as "days" in the first place.

Augustine warned Christians of his day that new scientific discoveries might overturn some theory they had rashly insisted was essential to the faith. His concern was not that Christians might look silly, but that the Bible itself might be discredited. His approach speaks to the importance of intellectual humility and patience in the theological enterprise, virtues evangelicals might cultivate more vigorously in contemporary debates over origins.

What about evolution?

Before we consider this question directly, we should first recognize the sociological and historical background of the debate. Much of the current storm surrounding evolution grew from a series of events in the beginning of the twentieth century called the Fundamentalist-Modernist Controversy that resulted in the division between mainline Protestant denominations and fundamentalist or evangelical groups.

After Darwin's *On the Origin of Species* was released in 1859, conservative Protestants like B. B. Warfield, a professor of theology at Princeton Theological Seminary and a staunch defender of biblical inerrancy, did not consider evolution a threat to historic Christian doctrines. Warfield thought evolution was compatible, for instance, with the position that all humanity descended from Adam. It was events like the Scopes trial of 1925, when ACLU lawyer Clarence Darrow made a mockery of fundamentalist representative William Jennings Bryan, that helped mark evolution as a kind of public dividing line between "liberals" and "conservatives."

As the two sides parted ways, mainline Protestant denominations increasingly abandoned classic tenets of Christian orthodoxy, and fundamentalist or evangelical groups withdrew from the life of the mind to preserve traditional beliefs. But the former also came to be associated with the urban, secular elite, and the latter with anti-intellectual conservatism. The result was a division both theological and sociological in nature. Thus, while there were genuine doctrinal differences that separated the two communities, personal suspicions played a role as well. Those who held to evolution were increasingly perceived as those who also rejected the supernatural, cared more about science than the Bible, were willing to compromise with the world and so forth. (There were, of course, stereotypes in the other direction.)

Addressing such flashpoint issues takes great nuance and care. Polemical caricature tends to produce more heat than light, and Christians often fall into the trap of demanding immediate answers to difficult questions. But God does not promise us comprehensive knowledge of the world (though he does give us everything necessary for salvation), and some intellectual problems take generations or even centuries for Christians to resolve. Christian humility means acknowledging the limits of our own competencies and recognizing where we might learn from others with more expertise. We should listen to scientists and resist drawing definitive conclusions on matters beyond our ken.

That said, I would suggest the following affirmations as theologically essential for a basic framework on the question of human origins. First, God is ultimately responsible for the creation and preservation of the world. God certainly uses means to accomplish his will—and such means may proceed in fits and starts—but he exercises final sovereignty over all that comes to pass. Second, humans are distinctly created in the image of God. How exactly the *imago Dei* should be defined, and how exactly we received this special status, are open for discussion; but Christians must affirm humanity's privileged condition over the animals. Third, the presence of suffering and evil in the world must be attributable to the free decisions of human agents. We may debate how to define suffering and evil, but we cannot believe God created the world badly, for that would be blaming evil on God.

These basic affirmations close off certain possibilities, but leave a number of others open. Some versions of evolutionary theory are clearly out of the question, including those that advance an atheistic, purely naturalist worldview. But other versions that can affirm God's guidance of the process and the miraculous character of humanity may not be incompatible with Scripture's teachings on creation. Given the range of intellectual options available for Christians on these matters and the dif-

The Scopes Trial. No event in American history so seared the perception of "fundamentalists" as rural, uneducated traditionalists as the celebrated "Monkey Trial" of 1925 in Dayton, Tennessee. The trial involved John Scopes, a young biology teacher, who was charged with teaching evolution in a public school. The American Civil Liberties Union supplied his legal defense, and William Jennings Bryan, a former Congressman from Nebraska and three-time presidential candidate, volunteered his services for the prosecution. In his cross-examination of Bryan, Clarence Darrow, the ACLU's lead attorney, exposed Bryan's inability to answer basic questions about the Bible and his ignorance of science and modern scholarship. Scopes was found guilty and fined one hundred dollars (though this decision was reversed on a technicality), but the fundamentalists lost the trial of public opinion. This moment was popularized in a number of plays and films, perhaps most famously by the movie *Inherit the Wind*.

ficulty of making absolute claims on events so removed from our direct experience, it would, I think, behoove evangelicals to exercise more restraint in this debate than we often have. As Christians, we should expect the world to find us curious, strange and even offensive. We would do well to avoid initiating battles that do not need to be fought.

Does God control everything that happens?

In short, yes. According to consistent scriptural testimony, as well as the broad consensus of Christian tradition, the scope of God's rule is as wide as the universe itself. Still, there are many complexities and controversies to this issue, and even a basic answer here will raise questions that will have to be addressed in other sections and chapters.

God's sovereignty includes the big and the small. On the one hand, Isaiah writes in sweeping terms, "'I make known the end from the beginning, from ancient times, what is still to come. I say, "My purpose will stand, and I will do all that I please." . . . What I have said, that will I bring about; what I have planned, that will I do'" (Isaiah 46:10-11). On the other hand, Jesus affirms God's care for the least remarkable events of nature. It is God, for instance, who causes the sun to rise and the rain to fall (Matthew 5:45); and God who feeds the birds and makes the lilies grow (Matthew 6:25-34).

God's sovereignty also encompasses suffering, evil and sin. According to the biblical authors, God struck David's child with illness and death (2 Samuel 12:15-18); brought about the loss of Job's livestock, servants and even children (Job 1); and took Ananias and Sapphira's lives because of their deception (Acts 5:1-11). At various points, we are told that God hardened Pharaoh's heart (Exodus 9:12); he incited foreign nations to wage war against Israel (Joshua 11:20); and he will send a powerful delusion in the end times to deceive evildoers and seal their condemnation (2 Thessalonians 2:11-12).

Such passages naturally make us wonder whether God is the author of evil. Yet Scripture denies this to be the case. As James tells us, "When tempted, no one should say, 'God is tempting me.' For God cannot be tempted by evil, nor does he tempt anyone; but each person is tempted when they are dragged away by their own evil desire and enticed" (James 1:13-14). God is not just holy; he is holiness itself. He therefore cannot be responsible for our sin.

How God can be sovereign over all things yet remain untainted by our sin is indeed a mystery, and it is no surprise that Christians through the centuries have wrestled with this issue in different ways. We are probing the profundities of the transcendent God, and none of us has all the answers.

I think we can, however, agree on the following foundational confessions. First, God exists at a different level of being and causation from our own. We tend to think of God in human terms, as if he were simply a stronger, wiser and more knowledgeable version of ourselves. But God is fundamentally other—the great I AM (Exodus 3:14)—and, as we have discussed, he transcends time. Quite a lot of our confusion as to how God governs the world can be traced to our inability to grasp what it means for God to be eternal.

Second, Scripture never depicts God as some sort of malicious tyrant, nor the course of human history as a manipulative game. God's sovereignty functions in Scripture as a source of comfort and security precisely because God is loving and merciful. We need not understand all the mysteries of providence to trust in God's goodness and overarching plan to bring about the healing and restoration of all things.

Third, Scripture's insistence on God's sovereignty never functions to lessen our ownership of our actions. Every command in Scripture presupposes our identity as free agents who are called to respond obediently to our Maker. We are not computers or robots acting out a script; we are image-bearers of God with the ability to choose our own path. However we construe the relation between God's sovereignty and our responsibility as free agents, we must affirm both.

How can we have free will if God controls all things?

Given the strong scriptural affirmations of God's sovereignty, it is natural to wonder whether any place is left for human agency. Indeed, even non-Christian philosophers have debated the nature of free will for thousands of years.

One common definition of free will is "the ability to choose otherwise." Suppose that you were at an ice cream store and had a choice between vanilla and chocolate. You choose vanilla, but you feel like you could have chosen chocolate if you had preferred. Free will would be fulfilled on this definition because the option of choosing another flavor was available to you.

While this definition may initially seem appealing, closer inspection reveals two problems. First, if we really could choose otherwise, it becomes difficult to affirm God's sovereignty over all things, let alone his knowledge of the future. How could God even predict what we are going to do if the possibility of alternative choices remains? Second, it is not clear that the ability to choose otherwise captures what we want to affirm in our basic intuition that we are responsible for our actions. Do the choices we feel are "ours" always involve some alternative option?

When I lived in Durham, North Carolina, there was a restaurant called Parker and Otis that boasted a remarkable shrimp BLT sandwich. The menu certainly had other good options, but they were irrelevant to me. I always ordered the same thing—to the point where the cashiers did not even have to wait for my order. "Shrimp BLT again with egg salad side?"

From a philosophical perspective, the key issue in those moments was not the opportunity to order a different sandwich, but the fact that I could order what I wanted. Nobody was forcing me to eat something else; my desires and my decision were perfectly aligned. Indeed, it would have felt somewhat odd to define freedom as my ability to order a different sandwich. Why would I want to choose *against* my desires?

This points us toward the heart of free will. Free will names the theological reality that we are creatures with dispositions and longings, and that we can make choices according to our own desires. To put it simply, we can do what we want. This understanding of free will does not answer every question about God's sovereignty, but it highlights a number of important theological dynamics.

First, as we have said above, divine sovereignty and human responsibility must both be true in a very strong sense. We are free agents, but we are not utterly independent or autonomous of God's rule. God oversees everything that comes to pass, but not in a way that nullifies our participation in his plan. The place in Scripture where this is seen most clearly is the cross. If we were not responsible for our actions, God would have had no reason to send his Son into the world, for our sins would be what God forced us to commit. Yet God's sovereignty also secures the cross, for Herod and Pontius Pilate did only what God ordained (Acts 4:27-28). The very narrative of redemptive history depends on a right understanding of this tension.

Second, the mystery of God's sovereignty and human responsibility must lie at the level of human desire. One curiosity about the exodus story is that the text says both that God hardened Pharaoh's heart (Exodus 9:12, as we saw above) and that Pharaoh hardened his own heart (Exodus 8:15). Theologians have sometimes sought to explain this phenomenon by understanding Pharaoh's hardening not as God's actively causing Pharaoh to sin, but as God's passively permitting Pharaoh to do as he pleased. A similar situation might be found in Romans 1, where God's giving people over to their natural desires results in all sorts of wicked behavior. While some theologians have sought other interpretations for these passages, it must somehow be the case that God directs our desires such that we choose as we please while acting as God has seen fit.

Third, though, there is a sense in which sin is not what we actually desire after all. Each of us has experienced this. We do something wrong and we know that we acted according to our own desires. But we also wish, somewhat paradoxically, that our desires were different from what they are. Paul describes this condition in Romans: "For what I do is not the good I want to do; no, the evil I do not want to do—this I keep on doing" (Romans 7:19). For Paul, this experience is a form of slavery, and liberation can only come through Jesus Christ. God has so oriented us toward himself that even when we act according to our desires by rejecting him, we cannot escape a deeper longing to be united with him in faithfulness and love. The richest and most biblical understanding of freedom, then, is not simply the ability to act according to our desires, but the ability to align our desires with God's will as slaves to righteousness (Romans 6:15-23).

Can we ever be outside God's will?

This is a question we all wrestle with at a personal and not just intellectual level. Does God have a plan for my life? Have I made the right decision? Will God restore my life after a major mistake? Is God angry with me?

Theologians sometimes distinguish between the *revealed* and *hidden* wills of God. The former can also be called God's "moral" will, and refers to what God teaches us to do. It is God's revealed will that we share the gospel with the lost, trust in God through prayer, heed his voice in

Scripture and give up our possessions to care for the poor. God's hidden will refers to God's overarching sovereignty over all things. We do not always obey God's revealed will, and human history is marked by instances of tremendous suffering and evil. Yet even these aspects of the created order must somehow fall under God's broader purposes. God's hidden will, then, includes much that is not part of God's revealed will.

In a sense, then, the answer to the question above is both yes and no. It is possible to be outside God's revealed will—by oppressing the poor, for instance, or rejecting the authority of Scripture—but we cannot, by definition, be outside God's hidden will. Such a distinction entails both a warning and a promise. On the one hand, God does grant us the freedom to make decisions, and a repeated pattern of active disobedience against God may well result in our final separation from him. Herod and Pontius Pilate acted according to the "will" of God, but we do not want to follow their example (Acts 4:27-28).

On the other hand, those who repent can take comfort that even the worst of our sins can be forgiven, and that our mistakes may in fact contribute to God's redemptive purposes. One of the odd features of the Christian life, and Scripture more broadly, is that times of suffering and sin can be renarrated in our ongoing progress as God's people such that failures become a source of joy and thanksgiving as they set forth more clearly the mercy of Christ. We should never sin for the sake of producing a better conversion story. But there is a retroactive and qualified sense in which we may even delight in sin for the glory its destruction brings to the Father.

It is the grace of Christ, then, that makes the psalmist's words a song of joy, which we too may recite: "Where can I go from your Spirit? Where can I flee from your presence? If I go up to the heavens, you are there; if I make my bed in the depths, you are there. If I rise on the wings of the dawn, if I settle on the far side of the sea, even there your hand will guide me, your right hand will hold me fast" (Psalm 139:7-10).

Has God already chosen the person I will marry?

Maybe, but don't get too worked up about this. In the first place, it may not be God's will for you to get married at all. This is not necessarily punishment. Paul wishes in 1 Corinthians 7 that more people had the gift of singleness he enjoyed, and the Christian tradition bears witness to many saints who have chosen celibacy as a special form of self-dedication to God. Protestants tend not to take this possibility as seriously as Scripture and tradition commend.

This Is My Father's World
Maltbie D. Babcock, 1901

This is my Father's world, and to my list'ning ears,
All nature sings, and round me rings the music of the spheres.
This is my Father's world: I rest me in the thought
Of rocks and trees, of skies and seas;
His hand the wonders wrought.

This is my Father's world, the birds their carols raise,
The morning light, the lily white, declare their Maker's praise.
This is my Father's world: He shines in all that's fair;
In the rustling grass I hear Him pass,
He speaks to me everywhere.

This is my Father's world, O let me ne'er forget
That though the wrong seems oft so strong, God is the ruler yet.
This is my Father's world: the battle is not done;
Jesus Who died shall be satisfied,
And earth and heav'n be one.

If it is indeed God's will that you get married, then yes, there is a broad sense in which he knows who that person is. God knows and ordains all things, after all, and his governance over the world certainly extends to marriage relationships. But here's the rub—God does not necessarily reveal such matters to us, and presuming he has can cause a lot of foolish behavior. I know of one woman who went to seminary and was soon approached by a fellow student who claimed, after much prayer and reflection, that it was God's will for them "to date with the potential for marriage." She took this line a bit less seriously when a second student approached her with the same divine conclusion. And by the third time, she began to wonder if this was simply the way male seminarians ask women out on dates!

The reason God does not always provide clarity on such matters is that he wants us to trust him. Our desire for absolute certainty can actually be a form of idolatry, an attempt to short-circuit the process of learning to follow God by demanding his gifts instead. We can also put too much pressure on others if we care more about whether someone is "the one" than about simply getting to know him or her as a person.

Reflecting on God's sovereignty assures us that his plans for us are good, but we should be wary of using this teaching to manipulate God or others. And it is much better practice to affirm God's will in bringing two people together after the fact—by practicing marital fidelity—than to base our decisions on premature predictions.

5

WHAT IS THE MEANING OF
EVIL AND SUFFERING?

Jennifer Powell McNutt

On December 14, 2012, a lone gunman entered Sandy Hook Elementary School and inexplicably mass murdered twenty children and several adults before taking his own life. Looking back, it is hard to believe that this heinous crime was not the most deadly but the second-deadliest school shooting in US history. With the Christmas season in full swing, the nation grieved like never before as pictures of victims aged six and seven were released. What became clear to all, in that collective moment of horror and despair, was that no place—not even Newtown, Connecticut—is safe from the most evil events of this world. Many ask in the face of such tragedy, where is God in moments like these?

There are numerous gut-wrenching experiences of evil and suffering in our world. Prior to Newtown and during my lifetime, the tragic event that stands out because of the way in which it altered world relations and dynamics is when al-Qaeda terrorists flew two commercial airliners into New York's World Trade Center towers. The towers soon collapsed and immediately killed about 3,000 people. I was a graduate student at Princeton Theological Seminary when New York commuters living in the city of Princeton lost their lives on that day, and I will never forget the fear, disillusionment and grief that so widely gripped all in its aftermath. As a seminary student, I was challenged to seek understanding without silencing the rightful place of lament in human life, trivializing the darkness of evil and suffering, mitigating the power and goodness of

God or diminishing the Christian calling to resist evil and to alleviate suffering in the world. Exceptional delicacy is required for this question because the matter at stake is not merely theoretical or philosophical, but concrete and visceral, touching each and every human life in particular ways and to varying degrees. Frankly, this task does not lead to simple answers, and it only takes another natural disaster, famine, epidemic, war, fatal accident, brutal assault or act of senseless violence to be reminded of the most pervasive question of our world.

Few theological questions are more important to current discussions about God. Since the turn of the twenty-first century, the bestselling literature of the "New Atheists," such as Christopher Hitchens's *God Is Not Great* and Richard Dawkins's *The God Delusion*, has generated controversy with its biting criticisms of religion. God's actions are likened to an abusive and violent tyrant by Hitchens. Likewise, Dawkins antagonistically describes the Judeo-Christian God as "jealous and proud of it; a petty, unjust, unforgiving control-freak; a vindictive, bloodthirsty ethnic cleanser; a misogynistic, homophobic, racist, infanticidal, genocidal, filicidal, pestilential, megalomaniacal, sadomasochistic, capriciously malevolent bully."[1] Underlying these conclusions lurks a driving question: how can God's existence and character be reconciled with the reality of evil in the world? Classically, this conundrum has required the affirmation of three propositions: (1) God is good; (2) God is all-powerful; (3) Evil exists—whether moral or natural evil. The New Atheists prefer to deny God's existence rather than to reconcile these claims. In this way, for some, belief in God largely depends upon the answer to the problem of evil.

The importance of the question is undeniable. The challenge of resolution, however, is due not only to the tension of the three propositions but to the pastoral dimensions of the question. As the Reformer Martin Luther once described it, believers stand at the overlap of two kingdoms. In this space, Christians experience the grief of this world in the face of evil and suffering while at the same time affirming the promises of Christian hope grounded in the resurrection of Christ (1 Corinthians 15:12-19; unless otherwise indicated all Scripture references in this chapter are from the New Revised Standard Version of the Bible). Yet, this hope is not merely eschatological but also transformational for the here and now. Following in the footsteps of Christ means addressing all dimensions of human life, including the spiritual, so that feeding the hungry with the bread of life occurs in more ways than one. With this action, believers not only continue to root their faith in Christ in the face of evil and suffering, but also importantly continue to *resist* evil and suffering. The Salvation Army recently conveyed this sentiment in an ad that stated, "We combat natural disasters with acts of God." The response of believers is not to accept destruction as the true path of this world but to recognize a fallen world in need of Christ yesterday, today and forever.

How can evil exist if God is good and all-powerful?

The origins of evil have largely been attributed by Christians to the willful disobedience of Satan and humanity from the very first parents. In early Christian theology, the abuse of human free will was stressed in the work of Augustine, who pointed to the disobedience of Adam as the cause for the perpetual corruption of humanity. Importantly, Augustine also understood evil to be an absence of good, rather than a substance at all, thereby completely denying God's creation of evil. Looking to the fall to answer this question has proven to be the most enduring historical response because it distances God from authoring evil, renders humanity inexcusable before God and highlights the mercy and goodness of God all the more. The question then is turned on its head by asking not *why* evil exists, but *how* good can exist.

What about natural evil? Does God cause earthquakes, tsunamis, famines, and cancer?

Based upon Romans 8:22-23, humanity and the rest of creation are linked in their fallen condition and their need for redemption: "We know that the whole creation has been groaning in labor pains until now; and not only the creation, but we ourselves, who have the first fruits of the Spirit, groan inwardly while we wait for adoption, the redemption of our bodies." This passage has been used to explain the cause of natural disasters in the world. Genesis further supports this interpretation by indicating that the once harmonious created order was corrupted after the fall along with humanity thereby alienating humanity from God, nature and one another. Consequently, the world no longer easily provides nourishment (Genesis 3:17) and, though there is much beauty, it can also be harsh and lethal.

This point is powerfully illustrated by the 2007 movie *Into the Wild*, based upon the true story of Emory graduate Christopher McCandless and his withdrawal from human civilization for a life of solitude in the wilds of Alaska. There, a romanticized view of nature met the harsh reality of the dangers of nature when cut off from human contact. Furthermore, the vulnerability of humanity to its natural surroundings was contemplated in the apologetic writings of Blaise Pascal. Pascal's *Pensées* describes human life as paradoxical for being the greatest of all creation and the most fragile at the same time. He believed the enigma of the "thinking reed" was inexplicable apart from knowing God as the source.[2] As the philosophical theologian Diogenes Allen explains, "Our doubleness keeps pressing us to recognize that we live in a vast universe, that we are frail and mortal, and yet we have a stubborn sense of significance, a greatness which cannot be utterly suppressed."[3] In this way, the human paradox should lead us to look to something greater than ourselves.

Interestingly, as prominent thinkers began to move away from a fallen creation framework during the age of Enlightenment, this also lessened their ability to explain the suffering caused by the natural world. Ques-

The Lisbon Earthquake. In 1755, an earthquake hit Lisbon that would never be forgotten. Numerous lives were lost due to the collapse of churches that Sunday morning. Tidal waves and fire soon followed, leaving the capital of Portugal in ruins and thousands dead. Noted philosophers like Voltaire and Jean-Jacques Rousseau picked up the pen to make sense of this new tragedy. Eventually Voltaire would write one of his most famous works, *Candide*, in response. Yet, neither the quandary of Voltaire's response nor the callousness of Rousseau's succeeded in shedding much light on a controversial issue.

tions over this matter had been brewing since the Reformation as prominent philosophical minds grew disillusioned by the violent conflict that erupted within a divided Christendom. Under the religious persecution of King Louis XIV, Pierre Bayle (1647–1706) fled France for Holland after the limited toleration of Protestant worship was fully rescinded in 1685 with the revocation of the Edict of Nantes. In the face of trying circumstances, Bayle's *Historical and Critical Dictionary* (1697) declared that the universe was not under the control of a good God. In 1710, the German philosopher Gottfried Leibniz (1649–1716) wrote the work *Théodicée*, a term he coined to represent a reply to the problem of evil. Leibniz contested Bayle by asserting that the world was the best of all possible worlds. The issue drew more attention when on November 1 of 1755 the Lisbon earthquake rocked the Iberian Peninsula and shook Europe to its ideological core. In the end, however, the optimistic regard of the era for human capability and admiration for the created order left little room for explaining events such as these.

Is evil and suffering punishment for sin?

Beyond identifying the fall as bringing evil into the world, Christians of the past and still today have affirmed that God's providence includes causing natural disasters or disease, and such events have been interpreted as God's righteous judgment for sin. The characterization of God in Scripture as the just judge (Psalm 7:11) informs this outlook. For this reason, the most common response of the church historically to occurrences of moral and natural evil has been repentance and fasting. The New England earthquake of 1727, for example, led to religious revival that precipitated the first publicized "awakening" prior to the Great Awakening that began with Jonathan Edwards.

However, this interpretation presumes to understand exactly how God works through current events and why. Also, it seems to demote if not deny the work of the devil in the world. As the nineteenth century French poet Charles Baudelaire would later write in his prose-poem, *The Generous Player*, "the cleverest ruse of the Devil is to persuade you he does not exist!"[4] For this reason, in David Bentley Hart's interpretation of the tsunami disaster of 2005 for *First Things*, he writes, "As for comfort, when we seek it, I can imagine none greater than the happy knowledge that when I see the death of a child I do not see the face of God, but the face of His enemy."[5] Indeed, the idea that God *causes* evil can be seen to conflict with God's goodness when Scripture defines the endgame of evil as "to steal and kill and destroy" (John 10:10). In contrast, Jeremiah 29:11 promises, "For surely I know the plans I have for you, says the LORD, plans for your welfare and not for harm, to give you a future with hope." In other ways, Scripture challenges a simplistic equation of suffering with sin. John 9, for example, recounts the story of Jesus and the blind man from birth. According to the text, "his disciples asked him, 'Rabbi, who sinned, this man or his parents, that he was born blind?' Jesus answered, 'Neither this man nor his parents sinned; he was born blind so that God's works might be revealed in him'" (John 9:2-3). The focus here is not on punishment at all but God's miraculous plan to bring sight to the blind.

In April 1912, Swiss theologian and pastor Karl Barth tempered a simplistic interpretation of punishment in his sermon by addressing the sinking of the Titanic. More than 1,500 lives were lost from that tragedy, and Barth sought to counter conclusions that this event proved the sinfulness of pursuing technological advancement. In contrast, he declared to his congregation, "We humans so easily become senseless and superficial when we have to speak about things like this, or else we make rash and presumptuous judgments, as if we had been sitting in the divine council when this incident was being ordained."[6] Instead, he rejected the idea that the sinking of the Titanic was an essential and inevitable part of God's plan, and he pointed out numerous ways in which events could have had a different outcome if, for example, there had been just as much concern for human safety as for generating revenue. This outlook resonates theologically with Barth's affirmation that God's sovereign will and humanity's actions are both at work in events. Thus, he recognized the sinful human decisions that led to the catastrophe as well as human acts of goodness that responded. For Barth, God's power and goodness were present in those who were self-sacrificing, such as the musicians who played to calm the panic and the men who allowed women and children to board life boats in their stead. He writes,

One senses something of how Christ is becoming an ever greater force in the world, when one reads of those who did not seek to save themselves but did their duty, who ultimately did all they could, not for themselves but for others, who silently and nobly retreated in the face of death to allow those who were weaker than them to continue on the path of life. . . . In the attitude and conduct of those ordinary sailors during the most severe hour of testing, we see once again a sign of the new heaven and new earth for which we are waiting.[7]

If God does not cause evil, is he at least in control of evil?

Even with an affirmation of the fall, understanding God's providence in relation to the occurrence of evil and suffering still continues to raise challenging questions. During the late nineteenth century, Fyodor Dostoyevsky's *The Brothers Karamazov* responded to the idea that God's providence entails causing evil events in the world. In the story, the character Ivan Karamazov grimly recounts the suffering and evil that befalls children; graphic crimes of abuse, torture, and malice fill the pages to the point that one can hardly read on. Disturbingly, this account conjures up the horror felt upon learning of the attacks on children at Newtown. With this raw association in mind, Ivan's assertion is even more provocative:

Imagine that you yourself are erecting the edifice of human fortune with the goal of, at the finale, making people happy, of at last giving them peace and quiet, but that in order to do it it would be necessary and unavoidable to torture to death only one tiny little creature, that same little child that beat its breast with its little fist, and on its unavenged tears to found that edifice, would you agree to be the architect on those conditions, tell me and tell me truly?[8]

Ultimately, Ivan's belief that evil is caused—indeed, necessitated—by God, leads to his rejection of God.

Yet, many Christians have denied God's role as the *cause* of evil and suffering. Some have instead affirmed God's role as passively *permitting* evil and suffering in a fallen world, as seen in the book of Job. John Calvin, for example, described the evil one as bridled by God. The assurance that God does not cause evil but controls evil ensures that evil and suffering are still ultimately governed by God's providence. The limiting of evil by the power of God not only explains the ongoing existence of good in the world but provides a more nuanced way of relating the three propositions. It is the assurance of God's final victory over evil that Process Theologians forfeit when they decide that it is better to limit God's power in the face of evil in order to maintain God's goodness and mercy. If God is passive in some ways, how is God active in the world?

If God permits evil, is he also simply passive in events of evil and suffering?

According to Scripture, despite the corruption, suffering and death of this world, the unmatched power and goodness of God is evident both in God's ability to transform human suffering and evil for good and in the promise that evil will never prevail in the end (Matthew 16:18). As the story of Joseph teaches in Genesis 50:20, "Even though you intended to do harm to me, God intended it for good, in order to preserve a numerous people, as he is doing today." Therein both corrupt human action and perfect divine action are at work but with intentions and results at total variance with each other. Rev. Dr. Martin Luther King Jr. made this point in his sermon after the Baptist church bombing that killed three African American girls in 1963, saying, "God still has a way of wringing good out of evil."[9]

God is able to use any opportunity for his good will. I've observed this in numerous ways throughout my own life. Most significantly for me, if the terrible death of my mother's first husband had not occurred, I would not have been born. Recognizing this has led me to further believe in the power of God as good, merciful and loving through God's ability to transform what is so totally dead and lost in despair and, against all odds, bring unexpected blessing and joy from it. This resonates with the promise of Romans 8:28 (NIV) that "in all things God works for the good of those who love him, who have been called according to his purpose." Ultimately, there is mystery to the work of God in the midst of evil events. Nevertheless, transforming a wrong into a right is the unfathomable work that God fulfills in this world. As Jesus declares in Matthew 19:26, "For mortals it is impossible, but for God all things are possible."

How does the cross relate to questions about evil and suffering?

In the wake of the staggering loss of life from World War II and the horror of the Holocaust or *Shoah* ("calamity"), Christian theology has tended to stress God's participation in human suffering. Jürgen Moltmann's *The Crucified God* employs this approach, and the intention to convey a compassionate, firsthand understanding of human difficulties also reflects the words of Hebrews 4:15: "For we do not have a high priest who is unable to sympathize with our weaknesses, but we have one who in every respect has been tested as we are, yet without sin." The emphasis on the suffering and death of Christ certainly gives an answer to the temporal grief that is felt when reflecting on the devastating events of world history. Yet, there is much more than sympathy offered here.

In the death and resurrection of Jesus Christ, fully human and fully God, the gospel definitively proclaims that God is the undoer of the evil and suffering of this fallen world. The awesome power and love of God in the face of evil is shown through God's action, literally, bringing life out of death. For this reason, Scripture advances an eschatological mindset, which renders pale even the greatest suffering of this world in comparison to the glory that will be known to believers (Romans 8:22-25). In the end, even the evil and suffering of this world cannot hide the truth that humanity needs the Savior; sometimes it takes the most heinous moments to shake a person awake to the true gravity of life. As C.S. Lewis's demon character Screwtape stresses in the satire *The Screwtape Letters*, "In peace we can make many of them ignore good and evil entirely; in danger, the issue is forced upon them in a guise to which even we cannot blind them."[10]

How else have Christians put a positive spin on the question?

Because Christian theology understands the incarnation of Christ as essential to overturning the consequences of the fall, as seen in the work of Athanasius, for centuries the fall came to be known in the West as the "happy fall." This outlook bears similarity to Holy Week's Good Friday. By this reasoning if it were not for the apple there would not be a cross; if it were not for the apple we would not know God the Redeemer.

Moreover, the church father Irenaeus couched the entire human story in a process of becoming with the maturation of the believer occurring through the difficulties of life. This mindset resonates with scriptural affirmations of God as disciplining teacher or father (Proverbs 3:11; Hebrews 12:5), the potter who shapes and forms clay (Isaiah 64:8; Jeremiah 18; Romans 9:21), and the silversmith who refines and purifies metal in the fire (Malachi 3:3). Each metaphor conveys the transformation of humanity through difficult processes. From this standpoint one can begin to understand the inexplicable joy that is conveyed in Paul's account of his own suffering for Christ in Romans 5:3-4 (NIV): "We also glory in our sufferings because we know that suffering produces perseverance; perseverance, character; and character, hope." These hardships are summarized in 2 Corinthians 11:24-28 where Paul recounts multiples lashes, beatings, a stoning, shipwrecks, dangers from nature and humanity, hunger, thirst, cold, nakedness and sleeplessness all for Christ. While in Philippi, he was attacked by a crowd for preaching, stripped of his clothes, beaten with rods and thrown into prison. Nevertheless, that night, with shackles on his feet, he and Silas prayed and sang hymns to God (Acts 16:16-34). Their rejoicing was so powerful that the prison itself was shaken open and the jailer of the prison was converted to the Christian faith.

The ability to rejoice in God no matter the circumstances is a powerful response that defies worldly understanding and expectations. This is because in Christ we discover who we are and who we are meant to be. Transformation begins through union with him, and our life and death is given a purpose that is far greater than this fleeting world (2 Corinthians 4:16-18), providing the ultimate hope in the most devastating of circumstances. The story of Horatio Spafford offers one such story. Spafford was a Presbyterian elder and successful lawyer in Chicago during the nineteenth century. Among other things, he was an important supporter of the evangelist Dwight L. Moody and of the abolitionist crusade. In 1871, the Great Chicago Fire broke out and destroyed Spafford's many real estate investments. Two years later Spafford decided to take his wife Anna and their four daughters to Europe for the benefit of Anna's health. When business unexpectedly kept him back in Chicago,

Spafford sent his wife and daughters on ahead of him instead. While crossing the Atlantic, however, their ocean liner was struck by another vessel, and their ship sank within minutes. All four of the Spafford daughters drowned, and soon after, Spafford received a telegram from Anna with the following words: "Saved alone." Spafford immediately left to collect his wife, who had landed at Cardiff, Wales. While crossing the Atlantic, his ship passed over the spot where his daughters had lost their lives. At that moment, he returned to his room and wrote the hymn, "It Is Well with My Soul." In a letter to Rachel, his wife's half-sister, Spafford wrote the following: "On Thursday last we passed over the spot where she went down, in mid-ocean, the waters three miles deep. But I do not think of our dear ones there. They are safe, folded, the dear lambs."[11]

Are Christians promised happiness when faithfully serving God?

Throughout the world, believers today are confronted with versions of the "Prosperity Gospel," which promises wealth, health and power to those who believe in God. For cultures dominated by materialistic pursuits as the source of ultimate happiness, this message of abundance has found numerous willing supporters. The promise of prosperity preys upon some of the most destitute and desperate in contexts such as Africa. Consequently, the Lausanne Theology Working Group (2008–2009) is one of many voicing opposition to a largely counterfeit message saying,

> the teachings of those who most vigorously promote the "prosperity gospel" are false and gravely distorting of the Bible . . . their practice is often unethical and unChristlike, and . . . the impact on many churches is pastorally damaging, spiritually unhealthy, and not only offers no lasting hope, but may even deflect people from the message and means of eternal salvation. In such dimensions, it can be soberly described as a false gospel.[12]

In the end, the success of this movement illustrates just how easy it is to misconstrue the happiness that Christians *are* promised when faithfully serving God according to Scripture.

Scripture teaches that the joy of the Christian life is fundamentally countercultural because it is not grounded in wealth or power; rather, faith in Christ is identified as the source of all joy for the restoration and new life that it brings as well as the eschatological hope that it promises. As 1 Peter 1:8-9 declares, "Although you have not seen him, you love him; and even though you do not see him now, you believe in him and rejoice with an indescribable and glorious joy, for you are receiving the outcome of your faith, the salvation of your souls." This joy is so rooted in the love of Christ that it is not subject to the cycles of fortune. On the contrary, more often than not, enduring the sufferings of this world is assured as part of what it means to pick up one's cross and follow Christ (Luke 9:23). As John Calvin wrote in his *Institutes* (1559), "Why should we exempt ourselves, therefore, from the condition to which Christ our Head had to submit . . . we share Christ's sufferings in order that as he has passed from a labyrinth of all evils into heavenly glory, we may in like manner be led through various tribulations to the same glory."[13]

There is no life in this world free from hardship, though hardships dramatically vary. Despite this variance, Scripture speaks of the establishment of a new order through Christ wherein the first are last and the last first (Matthew 20:16); wherein greatness is achieved through service (Mark 10:45); wherein love is offered to one's enemy (Matthew 5:44); and wherein even the smallest among us is given priority (Matthew 19:14). This truth is foolishness to the world as is the victory of the cross. As Paul wrote in 1 Corinthians 1:26-29 (NIV),

> Brothers, think of what you were when you were called. Not many of you were wise by human standards; not many were influential; not many were of noble birth. But God chose the foolish things of the world to shame the wise; God chose the weak things of the world to shame the strong. God chose the lowly things of this world and the despised things—and the things that are not—to nullify the things that are, so that no one may boast before him.

Rooting one's joy in Christ means discovering the source of true happiness from everlasting to everlasting that is not the happiness that the world seeks. Rather, whether in times of plenty or times of lean, Paul instructs Christians in Philippians 4:4-7,

Rejoice in the Lord always; again I will say, Rejoice. . . . Do not worry about anything, but in everything by prayer and supplication with thanksgiving let your requests be made known to God. And the peace of God, which surpasses all understanding, will guard your hearts and your minds in Christ Jesus.

How should Christians respond in word and deed to evil and suffering in the world?

Since the times of Plato and Aristotle, one of the classic philosophical affirmations of divine character has been God's inability to suffer and emote. Yet, even though "all the fullness of God was pleased to dwell" in Jesus (Colossians 1:19), when faced with the death of Lazarus of Bethany and the weeping of Lazarus's sister Mary, he was overcome with emotion for his dear friends and "began to weep" (John 11:35). In her book of sermons, *The Undoing of Death*, Anglican priest Fleming Rutledge explains that Jesus wept out of

> more than grief for Lazarus; this perturbation of spirit is caused by the presence of the Great Antagonist. God is revealing, through the Son, that he hates Death. . . . Jesus is deeply moved in spirit because he is gathering his forces for this mighty confrontation with . . . the Supreme Enemy of all that God has purposed. This is a truly cosmic duel. . . . But in the end, it is no contest.[14]

As Christians, following in the footsteps of Christ does not mean to dismiss the evil and suffering that we and others experience but to have compassion and to show solidarity with those who suffer. As Romans 12:15 instructs, believers are commanded to "Rejoice with those who rejoice, weep with those who weep." Thus, incidents of evil and suffering should not be dismissed, ignored or trivialized. Rather, first and foremost, believers bring their lament to God asking, "How long, O LORD? Will you forget me forever? How long will you hide your face from me? How long must I bear pain in my soul, and have sorrow in my heart all day long?" (Psalm 13:1-2). Yet, believers are not merely called to lament.

Consider again John 11. After Jesus mourned in solidarity with those grieving, he turned his attention to fulfilling the work that would bring glory to God—the undoing of death after the fourth day. Notice that first he prayed, thanking God for hearing him; then he commanded Lazarus to leave his tomb thereby calling him back from the dead. In that miraculous moment, not only did he raise a dead man from his grave, Christ also set in motion his own trial and crucifixion two miles away in Jerusalem: "So from that day on they planned to put him to death" (John 11:53). Similarly for Christians, preferential action for those suffering in this world must begin first and foremost with prayer, which seeks God's guidance in the discernment of every next step. The power of prayer should not be a neglected resource but should be repeated "without ceasing" (1 Thessalonians 5:17). Since there is no matter too great or too small for the power of God, believers must begin seeking the wisdom of God's will (Colossians 1:9) in the fight against evil and suffering.

Finally, prayer should lead to action. As Liberation Theology has shown, the resistance of evil and suffering in the world is modeled after Christ, who condescended to take on flesh (Philippians 2), fellowshipped with sinners and outcasts, fed the hungry, healed the sick and cared for

Liberation Theology. This contextual theology emerged from Latin America in the aftermath of the Second Vatican Council. Pope Paul VI met with Latin American bishops at Medellín in Columbia (1968). Due to political corruption, poverty and economic underdevelopment in the region, the bishops of Latin America demanded that the church give preferential treatment to the plight of the poor and oppressed. Theologians like José Miguéz Bonino stressed Christ's example of solidarity with the poor as the basis for Christian involvement in social and political action for the purpose of overcoming structural sin. This work was seen as central to a true proclamation of the gospel. For many of the leaders of the church who embraced this mission, the ultimate sacrifice followed. Most famously, on March 24, 1980, in the middle of saying Mass, Archbishop of El Salvador Óscar Romero was assassinated.

the poor. Likewise, the proper response of the Christian is to bring liberation that addresses both spiritual *and* physical needs because hope in the promise of the one who claims to be the "resurrection and the life" means ultimate transformation as well as immediate transformation. Thus, Lazarus was raised from the dead only to have to die again, waiting with everyone else for the final resurrection and transformation of the body. In this way, the story of Lazarus represents our own immediate regeneration in Christ that begins with faith but does not see complete glorification until the last days. Until that day comes, care for the poor, sick, weak, hungry, naked, outcast, orphan and widow through prayer, proclamation and action represents the most important response of the body of Christ in the face of evil and suffering.

6

WHO IS JESUS?

Gary M. Burge

For a number of years I have been involved in interfaith dialogue groups with Jewish and Muslim theologians. Two things have become clear. First, we share a great deal in common with these monotheistic faiths. Each of us (in one way or another) believes in the one God who revealed himself to Abraham. We share a remarkably similar understanding of the world and our duty under God as we live our lives every day.

Second, I have also learned that in almost every dialogue, we quickly part company on one topic: what we believe about Jesus Christ (or "Christology"). When Jesus' Messiahship surfaces, the tension among the rabbis is palpable. When we mention Jesus' divinity, the Muslim imams become nervous. And for dialogue to move forward, it seems that either we set aside Christology or limit Christian claims for Jesus. But as theologians have often agreed: Christology is *the doctrine* which is the distinguishing hallmark of Christian faith. For this reason, compromising this belief is something I cannot do.

This awkwardness came up in one of our Christian-Muslim meetings in Toronto recently. We often wish to pray together before meals but when the Muslims asked that we please not refer to Jesus (no more praying in "Jesus' name") suddenly the struggle of interfaith unity surfaced.

The Christians were divided. Some were willing to comply with the request. "Jesus didn't pray in his own name," they argued, "so we should follow him." I was the spoiler when I mentioned John 14:13 ("whatever you ask *in my name*") and at once we knew we were at an impasse. But the Muslims were divided too. Liberal Muslims said that it didn't matter. "We believe

Jesus was a prophet and we are simply honoring him." Conservative Muslims said everything was at stake. "To make Jesus divine is polytheism." Joining conversations like this puts you right back in the early centuries where our beliefs about Jesus Christ were in their infancy.

Christology is one of the distinguishing beliefs that sets us apart as Christians. We are making the astonishing claim that God revealed himself in the person of Jesus, a Jewish man from Galilee who lived in the first century. But how we explain this is vital and it is easy to misstep.

God did not simply speak *through* Jesus as he might speak through a prophet. Jesus was not merely an inspired man in whom divine wisdom could be heard. This is what my Muslim friends believe about him. We part company when I am compelled to say that Jesus was more. Humanity alone, even a perfectly-lived humanity graced with divine insight, is not an accurate description of what we mean when we discuss Christology.

Nor was Jesus a unique creature created by God for his purposes. Even if someone suggests that Jesus was the first and greatest of God's creations—his perfect masterpiece with no parallel in history—we would be compromising essential ideas about him. We press for an *eternal* union between the Father and the Son (some theologians prefer to refer to their *coexistence* and *coequality*). This is not merely a union of purpose as if Jesus and the Father shared the same goals. Theology texts refer to this as an "ontological" union (from Greek, *ontos* [to be]: a union of being or essence or substance).

We believe that God himself *appeared* in the life of Christ in a manner not seen before. Or more precisely, God appeared *as* a human person (not simply *within* a human person). Christ was not an emissary from God trying to change God's mind at the cross; Christ was God-with-us who had come to show God's mind. God became flesh (the incarnation) to show us thoroughly who God is (revelation) and to work on our behalf (redemption), reconciling the world to himself. These twin affirmations—revelation and redemption—are critical. The temptation in modern theology is to reject the possibility of revelation (and thus the particularity of Christ) or reject the decisive nature of his redemptive work (thinking that what we really need is insight, meaning and purpose—not salvation). Both ideas must not be lost.

Therefore we have in Christ the remarkable self-revelation of God, where his unity with God is not compromised (the Council of Nicaea, 325) and the fullness of his humanity is not restricted (the Council of Chalcedon, 451). Jesus is fully God (one person of three in the Trinity) and fully human (bearing two natures, human and divine). These are the

The Council of Nicaea. Early in its history the church hosted a number of "ecumenical councils" to resolve theological disputes. The Council of Nicaea was the first such gathering and six more were to follow. Within months of suppressing the eastern provinces, Constantine called together hundreds of bishops (the exact number is unknown) to resolve a growing theological faction that he feared might disrupt the theological unity he desired for his reign. They met in the town of Nicaea (modern Turkish Iznik) in May 325 and worked for three months to address the views of Arius and various other subjects (such as the true date of Easter). The council produced an orthodox confession (the Nicene Creed) that included four anathemas for Arius's teachings. The Nicene Creed we use today, however, is taken from a revision of the creed completed in 381 at the second council, called the Council of Constantinople I.

How did it all begin? In Alexandria, Egypt, the bishop (Alexander) had clashed repeatedly with Arius, a popular elder in the city. Arius argued that the *Logos* (or "Word") was one of God's creatures, above common creation to be sure, but nevertheless created; Alexander replied that the Logos was "coeternal" with the Father and shared the same substance with the Father (Greek, *homoousion*). When Alexander condemned Arius, demonstrations in favor of Arius broke out not only in Egypt but throughout the eastern empire. Popular teachers used the Bible to argue that the Son was subordinate to the Father ("there was a time when he [Christ] was not"). Arius's followers even sported clever songs that average people sang in the taverns.

Many theologians were alarmed at this whole state of affairs, including the emperor Constantine.

fundamental theological boundaries which have been set over the centuries and to hold to an orthodox Christology is to accept them.

There have been disagreements in Christian history over a variety issues. Some have been major, particularly in the churches in the eastern Mediterranean. For instance, some disagreed with Chalcedon's formula arguing that Christ had one nature instead of two (Monophysites, "one-nature") and these communities such as the Egyptian Copts, the Syriac, the Ethiopian Orthodox and the Eritrean Orthodox moved away from the Chalcedonian position. However in the last few decades (after 1,500 years of division), the leadership of Egypt's approximately eight million Coptic Christians are seeking reconciliation. They claim that the disagreement at Chalcedon was a "linguistic misunderstanding" and that they are not "Monophysites."

Other disputes did not bring dramatic schism—such as how Jesus' death on the cross completes his saving work. But in the main, the twin anchors of Nicaea and Chalcedon have found a widely held consensus: the meaning of Jesus Christ is found in his eternal union with the Father (and the Spirit) and his genuine (not feigned) assumption of full human life.

Did Jesus claim that he was the "Messiah"?

Messiah is a Hebrew term used widely in Judaism to refer to a person who might serve a saving role in Israel. It could be a variety of figures—and in the New Testament era the expectation had grown exponentially. Thanks to centuries of political oppression, many Jewish leaders sought political redemption and therefore models such as Moses or David figured significantly in this hope. As Moses defeated Pharaoh, so too the Messiah would restore Israel's fortunes and return the nation to its previous glories. Messianic figures were—like Moses or David—human actors called by God to accomplish something remarkable. Isaiah can even refer to the Persian king Cyrus as "anointed" (Isaiah 45:1) because he was appointed by God to lead Israel home from its Babylonian captivity.

Messiah literally means "anointed" in Hebrew and its Greek form is *Christos*. Judaism's hope was that the Spirit of God would powerfully anoint (Greek *chrio*) this leader to save the nation. Thus "Jesus Christ" is actually a confession that Jesus (the man from Nazareth) was the "anointed one" or the awaited Jewish Messiah. This means that "Christ" is not Jesus' surname—a suggestion I've heard more than once. It is an expression of faith.

At the very least, Jesus' baptism in the Jordan River signaled the Spirit's anointing of his life and work. But here too we must be clear: his baptism was not God *adopting* an otherwise excellent man to become his son (hence adoptionism). It was God's recognition (or revelation) to the world of who Jesus already was. "This *is* my beloved Son" (Matthew 3:17 ESV). However because of the stark political overtones linked to the term *messiah,* it was with some caution that Jesus used the title. It wasn't till Jesus asked his apostles to confirm his identity at Caesarea-Philippi in northern Galilee that he openly adopted it for himself (Matthew 16:15). However he still refrained from using it in public even after this.

The Jewish Messiah was never a divine person. The idea that there would be another independent divine "person" in heaven alongside God is unimaginable in Judaism because of its strict commitment to monotheism. That said, however, we do find in Jewish thinking the idea of a heavenly figure who in some manner would come to restore Israel (see Daniel and the apocryphal books Enoch and the Psalms of Solomon). And remarkably—here is the surprise—the name generally used for this person is "Son of Man," Jesus' favorite title for himself (used eighty-two times in the Gospels).

Jesus indeed saw himself as messianic (or anointed by God); he chose a term for himself that pointed to a heavenly identity no ordinary Jew would use, and he needed to empty the title *messiah* of its popular associations. Two examples of the latter come to mind. In Luke 4:16-30 Jesus came to his home synagogue in Nazareth and was a celebrated speaker. But then when he explained that God's interests exceeded the ethnic boundaries of Judaism (including Syria and Phoenicia) the crowd immediately turned on him and called for his death. In Mark 8:31 for the first time Jesus spelled out clearly that his mission would include his suffering and death. Even Peter could not manage it (Mark 8:32). In both cases we see Jesus reframing the understanding of messiah in terms not commonly accepted by his peers.

Did Jesus see himself as the divine Son of God?

The phrase "son (or children) of God" was commonly used in the Old Testament for the Israelites (Exodus 4:22) or more narrowly Israel's king (Psalm 2:7). The Hebrew idea implied a shared identity or purpose with a father or patron and in this case, it was God. So the Israelites were God's sons or children because they lived alongside him within his covenant.

However, in the Gospels Jesus exceeds this by claiming a unique connection to the Father not shared by others (Matthew 11:25-30). In some cases, Jesus does things only God should do such as forgiving sins (Mark 2:7). This implies that the Gospel writers know something that they can only imply in their stories: Jesus bore a uniqueness not seen anywhere else. In Matthew, Mark and Luke only others refer to Jesus as "Son of God," but in John, the title is used fully by others for Jesus (John 1:49) and by Jesus himself (John 10:36). But what these writers believe is clear. Mark opened his Gospel with: "The beginning of the gospel of Jesus Christ, the Son of God" (Mark 1:1 RSV).

In John's Gospel the phrase even emerges into something more. Jesus' claim here to be the Son of God does not mean merely an affiliation with God or a harmony with God's purposes. Jesus assumes tasks reserved for God alone and by functioning in this role, he is claiming something more. "The Father is in me and I am in the Father" (John 10:38). According to John, in Christ we are hearing a divine claim, that in some manner, Jesus is bearing the reality of God within himself and that Jesus is equal with God. According to John, this idea is at the heart of the Jewish leaders' opposition to him (John 5:18). In John 10:30 Jesus can even say "I and the Father are one" and this leads to charges of blasphemy. In John 14:9 he can tell Philip that when he sees Jesus he is seeing the Father! The Gospel can begin with a direct correlation between "the Word" (who is Jesus) and God (John 1:1) and end with Thomas calling Jesus "my Lord and my God" (John 20:28).

I think that perhaps this idea of divine sonship was extremely difficult for Jesus to convey to the public. Its implications were so profound and controversial—and Judaism was so keenly committed to monotheism in a Roman polytheistic world—that Jesus' fullest answer had to remain veiled for the wider public.

Arius. Arius was an elder in the church of Alexandria (250–336) and because of the deep controversies that followed his teaching, much of his biography is obscure. Arius was a committed follower of Christ. And in the years of the church's theological infancy wanted to work out the relationship between the Father and the Son. He knew the Bible thoroughly and believed that our first commitment was to monotheism (that there is one God). However he felt that pressing the divinity of Christ, or better, his unity with the Father, compromised this monotheism. To press the point, Arius taught that "there was a time when the Son was not." This meant that Christ was created.

As often happens, Arius was charismatic, well liked, and a compelling debater. And he was a *provocateur*. He called those who disagreed with him "polytheists" because they had made Christ into a second god. God was indivisible and so to share his divinity with another compromised his oneness. And he believed the Bible was on his side. His favorite verses for the indivisible unity of God came from Deuteronomy 6:4; 32:39; John 17:3; and 1 Corinthians 8:6. His favorite verses for the subordination of the Son came from John 14:28; 1 Corinthians 15:28; and Mark 13:32.

Arianism was wildly popular. And despite its defeat at the Council of Nicaea in 325, variations of it continued to spread throughout the Roman Empire. It was addressed again at the second council of 381. But distant rural areas remained unconverted and it was popular among German tribes in the north. Eventually by the sixth century, Arianism was rare.

The virgin birth. Really?

Few elements in the story of Jesus' life inspire more raised eyebrows. For skeptics who want to criticize the Gospels, this claim is fertile ground for a great deal of late night cynical humor.

It is interesting how little attention this story received in the early church. Mark's Gospel does not refer to it. Neither does John. And curiously in all of the sermons in the book of Acts and in all of Paul's letters, there is no hint of it. My own theory is that it was as difficult to explain in the first century as it is today. This was a Roman world with full blown mythologies of gods cavorting with humans, often males with females. I imagine Christian preachers in the first century tried to stay as far away from that set of ideas as possible.

Nevertheless—perhaps at the insistence of Mary, the mother of Jesus?—the story of Jesus' birth was told years after his death. And Matthew and Luke faithfully recorded it. I am impressed with a number of things. These two Gospels are remarkably modest in how they handle the story. There are few details and they do not indulge in speculation about the processes at work. We are not told how Mary became pregnant but only that it happened.

With many such doctrines it is useful to explore what is at stake by considering its denial. At stake here is our understanding of the nature of what happened in Christ. Without any sense of incarnation (that God *himself* here entered our human story) Jesus Christ becomes the highest development of humanity with all of its potential. But this undermines the essence of the church's theological message. The gospel is not a human effort, however it may be inspired by God. The gospel announces a divine interruption of human affairs. It offers a word from afar, not a word from within. It says that God himself appeared through the womb of a woman to bring a divinely worked solution to the predicament of humanity ("the Word became flesh and dwelt among us," John 1:14 ESV). This is why the ancient theologians defended such phrases for Mary as "God Bearer" (Greek, *theotokos*, or as it became in Latin, *Dei Genitrix* or *Mater Dei*) to express the mysterious, incomprehensible event that took place in Bethlehem. Jesus was not an ordinary child. And his unprecedented origin (he is "Immanuel," God with us) is precisely what the virgin birth is expressing.

Was Jesus really tempted? Could he have sinned?

Getting a handle on this question requires that we take a detour. It would be easy to claim that because of Jesus' exhaustive embrace of our humanity, he *must* experience temptation in order to share in our experience. Certainly Hebrews 2:18 and 4:15 make this claim. But the problem we run up against is here: Within us there is an inevitability to our sin that Jesus did not share. Jesus is like us; but he is also unlike us. So a detour is necessary.

It is helpful to think about Adam in three stages of moral development. I can imagine Adam before the fall, Adam after the fall and Adam when he joins God in his resurrection. (1) Before the fall, Adam had the capacity to sin but was not bound by its inevitability. In other words it was possible for Adam not to sin. But he chose to do so and it was a true and genuine decision. (2) After the fall, we believe that sin then became an inevitability. It was not possible for Adam not to sin since sin worked its way into the very fiber of his moral being and quickly spread to all of humanity (see Romans 5:12-21). Our lives today are lived with this inevitable sinful tendency. Adam gave us our propensity to sin—and we indulge what we have been given. (3) The promise of our final redemption in heaven is our full restoration when we are fully sanctified and renewed by God. And here we can say that sin itself will be defeated. Our transformation will be so complete that we will not even be inclined to sin or we might say, it will not be possible to sin. Sin's inevitability will be gone. It may have been Augustine who provided this suggestion based on Adam and it is well worth remembering his threefold formula: (1) possible not to sin; (2) not possible not to sin; (3) not possible to sin. Christ may belong to the first.

Jesus' temptations were thus like that of Adam before the fall. As Adam was surely tempted, so too, Jesus was tempted. But unlike Adam, Jesus prevailed. Thus Jesus shares with us all aspects of our humanity without the inevitability of sin. Jesus defeated sin precisely by being genuinely tempted and overcoming this temptation. There was a possibility of Jesus sinning—because he was fully human—yet, there was an impossibility of Jesus sinning because he was empowered and guided by the Spirit to such an extent that he did not sin.

Did Jesus genuinely experience temptation? Yes. His union with our humanity requires this. Therefore he can sympathize with our experiences of temptation. The theological mistake at this point is to so underscore the divinity of Christ (in order to uphold his perfection) that we lose touch with the fullness of his humanity. And this is the critical point surrounding the Chalcedonian debates. If the unity of God and humanity in the incarnation is explained by eliminating Jesus' human soul (Greek *nous*) or perhaps requiring that his humanity subordinate itself so completely that it is like a "drop of oil" placed in the ocean (it is there, but meaningless), then we have erred. A genuine humanity is as vital as a genuine divinity when we think about Christ.

Is Jesus' divinity more important than his humanity?

In the first four centuries of the church, Roman culture was quite happy to affirm Jesus' divinity. The Greek and Roman worlds had a pantheon of gods and easily absorbed new claimants to divine status. In this era, it was Christ's humanity that provided the problem. Today much modern theology reverses this concern. Many would like to make Jesus into a mere man—an inspiring man perhaps—but nevertheless a human like each of us. Among evangelicals, the ancient concern remains.

This balancing act between divinity and humanity (and the importance of both) was one of the earliest critical decisions of the church. After the Emperor Constantine moved the capital of the empire from Rome to Byzantium (his "new Rome" renamed after himself: Constantinople), a deeply divisive argument broke out between those who wanted to deny Christ's full equality with God (Arians) and those who would affirm it. The division was so threatening that Constantine himself called a major meeting in 325 to resolve it. The creed they wrote, "The Nicene Creed" (revised in 381 at Constantinople), delicately and forcefully affirmed the critical value of Christ's true divinity. To cite the creed, Christ was of "one substance or essence" (*homoousios*) with the Father and fully made human in the incarnation (or in Greek, "made flesh," *sarkothenta*). Chalcedon sharpens it even more: Christ was "one essence" (*homoousios*) with the Father regarding his divinity *and* "one essence" (*homoousios*) with us regarding his humanity.

Humanity and divinity are therefore two essential commitments we use to navigate our way and each has equal importance. Perhaps the most important framer of this issue was Athanasius, a fourth-century Egyptian cleric who served as his bishop's secretary during the Council of Nicaea when he was twenty-seven. At thirty he became bishop of Alexandria and despite some years of exile, provided the church with forty-five years of theological leadership. (Eastern Orthodox Christians refer to him as the Father of Orthodoxy while his peers, such as Gregory of Nazianzus, sometimes referred to him as The Pillar of the Church.)

Athanasius became an outspoken defender of Nicaea after the council and argued that two doctrines are anchored to a clear understanding of

Athanasius. Behind the scenes of the great Arian controversy was a young man who would become one of the greatest theological minds of the fourth century. Athanasius was an Egyptian deacon who worked for the bishop of Alexandria prior to the Council of Nicaea. As a young man, he was drawn to the desert monasticism of Egypt and even knew St. Anthony, the founder of Egyptian monasticism (see his *The Life of St. Anthony*). Athanasius's book, *On the Incarnation of the Word*, penned before Nicaea, already showed astonishing promise.

As conflicts with Arius grew in Alexandria, Constantine called the first ecumenical council at Nicaea in 325. As a deacon (and the bishop's secretary), Athanasius attended the council but was not "seated" at the council like the other bishops. But we can assume that many sought his counsel.

After Nicaea, Athanasius went on to become the opponent the Arians most feared. He wasn't articulate nor did he possess political savvy. It was his monastic rigor, his integrity and love for his people (with whom he could speak fluent Coptic), and his indomitable, resolute spirit that made him unstoppable. Three years after Nicaea (328) his friend and bishop, Alexander, was on his deathbed and he earnestly wanted Athanasius to become his successor. The young man, now thirty, had no interest and fled to a desert monastery. But he returned reluctantly (to serve the church) and that year he became Alexandria's new bishop.

the humanity and divinity of Christ, particularly in his incarnation: revelation and redemption. Without divinity, the word spoken by Christ is a human word, not a word from God; it is a word "from below" and limited in its creatureliness. And without divinity, the effort of the cross would likewise be a human enterprise, another sacrifice not unlike those at the Jewish temple. But no. The revelation we possess in Christ is a divine word, a word "from above," a word originating with God himself. This makes it a unique word that bears unparalleled revelatory authority. But likewise, affirming Christ's divinity means that what transpired on the cross was God reconciling the world to himself (2 Corinthians 5:19). Salvation then is not a human effort accepted by God; salvation is a divine effort given to humanity as a gift.

But likewise Athanasius taught that without Christ's full humanity these two doctrines also fail. The success of revelation, its capacity to unveil the mysteries of God, requires that it come to us in creaturely form. Simply put, a divine word that does not accommodate the ears of its hearers cannot be heard. It is Christ's humanity, his full humanity, woven into the everyday world of the first century, that made average people understand and respond. And equally, the success of our redemption is hinged to our humanity—not a feigned humanity—but a genuine humanity sacrificed on the cross. At Golgotha Christ presented to the Father a humanity he truly embraced.

Athanasius's chief nemesis throughout his life were the followers of Arius (whom he labeled "Arians"). Arius knew the Bible well and like modern Jehovah's Witnesses (who are modern Arians) he could interpret the scriptures adeptly. Athanasius believed that avoiding the Arian error was critical not simply because of what Scripture taught but because of how a nuanced understanding of divinity and humanity—an orthodox Christology—was central to the working of Christian theology itself.

Did Jesus struggle with sexual temptation?

This answer follows on the foregoing. When we think about Jesus and sexuality we often become squeamish. If Jesus enjoyed a full humanity—as we claim he did—then I expect he was a man with all of those features that make a man what he is. He grew through puberty, his hormones were healthy, and he experienced a natural healthy appreciation for women. His candid reference to lust in Matthew 5:28 tells me he understood these things.

Our chief problem is that we have associated sexuality with sin. And just as Christians need to redeem our understanding of godly sexuality for ourselves, perhaps we need to recover some sense of Jesus' own sexuality. Jesus possessed every sexual capacity and interest *but without sin.* This means (as I noted above) that Jesus also experienced sexual temptation *without* its inevitability. He was a man whose sexuality was not impulsive or indulgent, but fully controlled by his desire to please God and his sincere respect for women. Jesus was never promiscuous. He possessed a deeply virtuous sexuality.

What did it mean to have a "virtuous sexuality" in ancient culture? Jesus lived in a world of arranged marriages. Casual informal interaction between unrelated men and women was sharply limited. Therefore it is unlikely that Jesus ever had opportunities for contact with women the way we imagine it today. Therefore we do not want to project ideas of male-female intimacy on his world. However I imagine Jesus also understood that his life in this area was going to be different than the rest of his male friends. In Matthew 12:49-50 Jesus astounds his audience when he claims that even his own family relations are different ("Who is my mother? And who are my brothers?"). He even believes that the call of his disciples will affect the usual affairs of family and home (Matthew 19:29). But does he understand marriage and respect it? He does. His open discussions about divorce and adultery signal his respect for marriage and his desire to preserve its purity.

When Jesus walked into a room, could he read everyone's mind?

Once we affirm the notion of the divinity of Christ, it is easy to pursue its implications to their logical end. If the Son shared essential attributes with the Father, then did he bring these into his incarnation? Was he omniscient? Omnipotent? Did he experience limitations?

Initially Scripture gives us a hint of our solution. In Mark 13:32 Jesus openly admits that he is ignorant of the timetable of the end times. "But of that day or that hour no one knows, not even the angels in heaven, nor the Son, but only the Father" (RSV). Therefore it seems that Jesus experienced genuine limitations despite the fact that he was the Son of God. A full experience of humanity points to those features that make us fully human. And limitation is one of them. As we cannot read someone's mind, so too, neither could Jesus. If this is true, we must read certain Gospel texts with some care. Matthew 9:4; 12:25; and Luke 9:47 each say that in some manner Jesus "knew" the thoughts of those with him and for some Christians this is a sign of his divinity or omniscience. Some would point to Jesus' anointing by the Spirit as the source of this remarkable ability. Still others prefer to see this as some indication of Jesus' Spirit-given intuition. He knows people so exhaustively he is able to deduce what is transpiring within them. John 2:24-25 might supply evidence of this: "But Jesus would not entrust himself to them, for he knew all people. He did not need human testimony about them, for he knew what was in them" (TNIV).

A related field of questions that turns on limitation is similar: Did Jesus ever make a mistake and get lost? Did he have to learn carpentry in Nazareth or was he born with these skills? If Jesus had to learn *anything* doesn't this imply human inadequacy on his part? Jesus had to learn. And in matters that were incidental—such as following the wrong path to Capernaum—he would exhibit true creaturely limits. In Nazareth he had to ask Joseph the angle of a saw cut *because he did not know.* And when he made a mistake and cut the wood wrong, Joseph showed him how to do it. This is what it means to be human. So Luke 2:52 tells us: Jesus *continued* to grow in wisdom.

The key here is working out the Chalcedonian relation between humanity and divinity. We have already seen that both ideas are critical. But how did they work together? The orthodox Christological solution is to say that in Christ we have one person in whom there are two natures (his "hypostatic union"). And these natures are successfully united (Chalcedon: Undivided! Inseparable!) but also not confused—retaining a genuine reality apart from their opposite. In some manner then the limitations of Christ are keyed to the reality of that human nature.

But when we have tried to advance this explanation, we are at once alert to the ease with which humanity and divinity might be misrepresented.

Some have suggested that in the incarnation Christ was different than he was from eternity. Christ emptied (Greek, *kenosis*) himself of his divine nature in order to enter our world and this explains his limitations. This view finds its support in passages such as Philippians 2:5-11 and to a degree it must be true. To embrace a creaturely life must mean the loss of some aspect of divine life in the incarnation. This seems true but how it is true remains unclear. Others have said that Christ did not lose his divine abilities at the incarnation but chose not to use them. The worst view would be to hold that in some manner the Son's ignorance is tied to his subordination to the Father or that the Father withheld this information from him.

The defenders of orthodoxy knew that they could not partition Christ and so blame his humanity for his limitations. His humanity and divinity were inseparable. To do so would mean that in his incarnation there was no complete and satisfying union of God and humanity (only a partial union since his bodily life would not touch his divine life) and if God has not joined our humanity in its deepest sense, then we have lost much of the mystery of God's saving work in the world.

When did Jesus save us?

It would be easiest to say simply that Christ died for our sins on the cross (1 Corinthians 15:3). And this would be true. But I also wonder if there is not more to this answer. The Greek notion of salvation (Greek, *sozo*) refers to making something whole that has been broken. In this sense, the work of salvation is a work of restoration, returning us to that place where God had always intended us to be. And forgiveness of sin is an essential component of that restoring.

If this is true, then it is also true that the entirety of Christ's work—his incarnation, his physical ministry, his death, his resurrection and his ascension—contributed to this restoration and salvation. In other words, God's entry into this world (the incarnation) began God's revelation and participation in our human affairs. His embrace of our humanity, his bearing it to the cross, and his holding it in his ascension, these too are works that are in place to bring us our salvation. In descent and ascent, Christ's every effort has been a saving effort to restore us to the life we have lost through sin.

Evangelicals tend to be "crucicentric," which means "centered on the cross." And we fail to see the comprehensive nature of Christ's work. As the early Christian bishop Irenaeus once argued, Christ moved through all stages of human life and experience and in this sense, *recapitulated* the life lived by humans. His holy obedience at every stage of human life created the possibility of a perfect humanity which he presented to the Father in his ascension. In his saving work, Jesus then became the author of a restored human race, something the world had never seen before.

Should I pray to Jesus or to God?

The simplest answer is to say that we should do as Jesus instructed us: Pray to God the Father (Matthew 6:9). However as Christians we remember that we pray to the Father through Jesus' name (John 14:13-14). And we know that the Spirit cooperates with our prayers, empowering them and helping them (Romans 8:26). Moreover we have examples in scripture of people like Stephen who pray to Jesus himself (Acts 7:59).

However, this question suggests a fundamental category mistake. It may imply that we believe the Father and the Son live separate lives and that connection to one would not mean connection to the other. Jesus Christ was the self-revelation of the Father. The life of the Son is found within the life of the Father. Or more succinctly, Jesus is God (understood as Nicaea has taught us). And therefore our prayers cannot be directed to the Father as if the Son could be absent. Christian prayer is always prayer mediated through the Son.

Because we believe in the trinitarian life of God, prayer to the Son implies that we are also praying to the Father. To see the Son is to see the Father (John 14:9). Therefore speaking to the Son is tantamount to speaking to the Father. The Father and the Son share one divine life (they do not coexist with two divine lives) and therefore our worship and our prayers address and glorify the unity of God as Father, Son and Spirit.

When I arrive in heaven, will I see Jesus—or the Father?
Or both?

This is the same question. For many younger Christians this question has

The Council of Chalcedon. The fourth ecumenical council was held in 451 at the city of Chalcedon near Byzantium. The full divinity of Christ had been upheld at the first two councils (Nicaea in 325, and Constantinople I in 381) but it remained to explore the full nature of Christ's humanity and how this humanity was related to his divinity. The Western church (thanks to Tertullian) was content to say that the two natures were simply united in one person. It was the eastern church where divisions flared.

Two views were debated: (1) One view (labeled Alexandrian) was willing to compromise Christ's humanity and even replace it with the divine Logos. Apollinarius of Laodicea had tried this earlier but his views were rejected at the second ecumenical council. However a monk from Constantinople, Eutyches, revived similar views in the fifth century by claiming that while Christ was "one substance" with the Father, he was not "one substance" with us in his incarnation. Essentially Christ had "one nature" (hence: *monophysitism*).

(2) The second view (labeled Antiochene) saw the teaching of Eutyches as docetic: Christ *appeared* human but was not. Nestorius (the bishop of Constantinople in 428) offered an alternative. Both natures (divine and human) could live side by side in Christ as two persons and never be confused. But making Christ "two persons" troubled many. It seemed that the unity of the two natures of Christ was at risk.

The third ecumenical council, which met at Ephesus in 431, failed to bring consensus because while Nestorius was condemned, he arrived after the council ended and could not defend his views. In 451 more than five hundred bishops gathered at the Council of Chalcedon. They upheld both the full humanity and full divinity of Christ that stand together in one person without confusion, without change, without separation or division. This essentially was the teaching of Tertullian two centuries earlier.

Many in the eastern church disagreed with this result and went their own way. For example, we know of churches from

Baghdad to Tibet and even China that were fully Nestorian through the fourteenth century. Today the Assyrian Church of the East is a remnant of this movement (although its bishop recently repudiated Nestorianism in 1976). Modern Alexandrian Christologies can be found today among some Christians in Ethiopia, Egypt and Syria. And Antiochene Christologies today can be found in northern Iraq and Iran. But at Chalcedon a major rift was complete: many Middle Eastern churches (Coptic and Syriac) and the Western churches (Greek and Latin) had parted ways.

a profound existential quality. The notion here is that the Father and the Son are significantly separate, the Father is problematic and perhaps angry, and Jesus has stepped in to be our defender. Therefore if we meet Jesus in heaven, he will give us cover when we meet the Father.

But this misses the basic point of Nicaea. Jesus came to reveal the Father, not appease an implacable Father. *"God was in Christ reconciling the world to himself"* (2 Corinthians 5:19). When we come to heaven we will meet Jesus Christ—who is the presentation, the revelation of God to us. And if we ask "What about the Father?" we will receive the same answer that Judas received in John 14. "Anyone who has seen me has seen the Father. How can you say, 'Show us the Father?' Don't you believe that I am in the Father and that the Father is in me?" (John 14:9-10).

7

WHAT IS SALVATION?

Keith L. Johnson

A few years ago, I drove through the worst thunderstorm I have ever experienced. I was on a two-lane highway late at night, and even though I knew the road and every landmark on it by heart, I felt lost. The beams of my headlights seemed to vanish in the sheets of rain, and I could barely see the road ahead. Limbs, leaves and other objects were flying through the air. The sound was intense, with the roar of the rain and the plinks of hail rattling the metal of my car. I thought for a moment that I was in the middle of a tornado. I considered pulling over, but the road did not have a wide shoulder, and I worried that someone might crash into me from behind. I tried my best to follow the reflective lights along the side of the road as my headlights caught them, but I quickly lost confidence. Was I actually in the right lane? Do yellow reflectors mark the *edge* of the road, or the *center* of it? In the moment, it was hard to remember. My only help was the lightning flashes across the sky, since they brought enough illumination to help me gain my bearings. I remember praying for help, my hands gripping the steering wheel tightly as I made my way home.

As I reflect upon this experience, I wonder if my feelings that night are similar to how many believers feel about their Christian lives a lot of the time. We know that the Christian faith is centered upon God's act to save us from sin and death through Jesus Christ and the Holy Spirit. Yet we also know that God's act carries implications for our everyday lives. After all, the earliest believers called Christianity "the Way" (Acts 9:2), and they knew that the Christian faith was just as much a way of life as it was a set of beliefs. But following the way of Jesus is *hard*. Jesus himself said that his followers must "deny themselves and take up their cross daily" (Luke 9:23).[1] Paul likewise often described the Christian life as a struggle, insisting that we must work hard to imitate Christ and "press on toward the goal" to which we have been called (Philippians 3:14). This goal and the difficulty it involves sometimes leads to frustration and even fear. As the debris of our daily lives whirls around us, we wonder: didn't Jesus promise "life to the full" (John 10:10 NIV)? If so, why do many of us still struggle with obedience on a daily basis? Shouldn't salvation mean freedom from sin and evil rather than a life spent fighting against them? Why are we still struggling to find our way through the darkness? Why would Christ expect us to "take up our cross" and follow him if salvation is by *grace*? And why does following Jesus often seem like we're driving through a storm, holding on to our faith for dear life?

These kinds of questions require good theological thinking. We will be able to work through them only when we can connect God's act to save us directly to our daily experience of the Christian life. We surely need to understand why we need salvation, the identity of the one who saves us and how salvation happens. Yet we also need to have a clear sense of both the purpose of our salvation and the concrete difference that "being saved" actually makes for our daily lives. The connection between God's act of salvation and our everyday lives will help us know why our obedience to God matters. It also will give us hope and courage as we follow the way of Christ in the midst of the storms that come our way.

Why do we need salvation?

The best way to understand our need for salvation is to compare our present situation to God's original intention for us. God created us in his own image with the task of exercising "dominion" over the earth (Genesis 1:26-28). Among other things, this task meant we are designed to reflect God's qualities and character by affirming what he affirms, denying what he denies and manifesting his righteousness and holiness in our words and deeds as we work, play and rest. This kind of life would glorify God because it would "image" God's own love, joy and peace in our posture toward him, one another and creation.

Because of our sin, however, we live in contradiction to God's intention. Rather than embracing God commandments, we disobey them and go our own way. This not only leaves us guilty of disobedience, but it also alienates us from God. Our sinful actions effectively call God's character into question, because they demonstrate that we do not trust that what God has said is true. Through our sin, we make ourselves God's "enemies" (Romans 5:10), and we deserve God's judgment. God exercises this judgment, in part, by simply turning us loose to pursue our twisted desires (Romans 1:24). The consequences of our self-rule are disastrous: relationships meant to be intimate exist under strain, work designed to be enjoyable becomes burdensome, and the dark spiritual "powers" confront us at every turn (Ephesians 6:12). Worse still, God's ultimate judgment against our sin is death (Romans 6:23). The first death is physical, and this is followed by the "second death," which takes the form of an eternal separation from God (Revelation 20:14; 21:8).

As sinners separated from God, the cloud of death hangs over every area of our lives, and we exist in desperate need. We need to be reconciled to God so that we can live in relationship with him once again. The guilt acquired from our sin needs to be forgiven and then taken away, so that we no longer stand condemned. We need to be freed from the burden of the evil powers that stand against us, and we also need to be transformed so that we actually reflect God's qualities and character in our being and in the way that we live our lives. Finally, we need victory over death in both its forms so that we might live with God eternally.

How does salvation relate to "the gospel"? What is the gospel?

Due to our sin, we need salvation. The Greek word behind "salvation" is *soteria*, a term used when something that has been broken, lost or sick is restored and made whole again; it describes an act of deliverance to safety. The term "gospel" comes from *euangelion*, which was used in the ancient world when a herald made a proclamation of "good news." While the two terms are closely related in Christian theology, they are not interchangeable. We can get a picture of their distinction and relationship by looking at one of Paul's best-known statements: "I am not ashamed of the gospel; it is the power of God for salvation to everyone who has faith, to the Jew first and also to the Greek" (Romans 1:16). Here the gospel leads to salvation, which comes as a consequence of it.

The gospel is the good news about the identity and action of Jesus Christ. Paul describes it as the "gospel concerning his Son, who was descended from David according to the flesh and was declared to be Son of God with power according to the spirit of holiness by resurrection from the dead, Jesus Christ our Lord" (Romans 1:3-4). The *news* is that God's Son has come in the flesh as the true heir of David, the long awaited Messiah of Israel. This news is *good* because of God's Old Testament promises that he would use Israel's Messiah to bring salvation to all peoples by atoning for their sin and giving them new hearts capable of obeying him. This is precisely what Jesus accomplishes in his role as "the Christ" ("the Messiah").

His actions are described by Paul in one of the clearest summaries of the gospel:

> That Christ died for our sins in accordance with the Scriptures, that he was buried, that he was raised on the third day in accordance with the Scriptures, and that he appeared to Cephas, then to the twelve. Then he appeared to more than five hundred brothers at one time, most of whom are still alive, though some have fallen asleep. Then he appeared to James, then to all the apostles. Last of all, as to one untimely born, he appeared also to me. (1 Corinthians 15:3-8 ESV)

The key saving actions in this passage are that Jesus "died for our sins," was "raised on the third day," and then appeared to the apostles who now testify about who he was and what he did. According to their testimony, recorded throughout the New Testament, Jesus brings salvation because his death and resurrection free us from the guilt and condemnation resulting from our sin, reconcile us to a right relationship with God and mark the defeat of death and the evil powers. This salvation becomes "effective through faith" (Romans 3:25), so that anyone who has faith in Jesus can be saved regardless of who they are or what they have done. Faith comes through the power of the Holy Spirit, who is sent by Christ and his Father to testify to Christ so that we may believe in him (John 15:26; 2 Corinthians 4:13).

It is important to keep the distinction between the gospel and salvation in view, because a blurring of it can lead to confusion about what salvation involves. For example, sometimes Christians talk about the "the gospel" as if it were identical to "how we get saved." This tends to shift our focus away from the *substance* of the gospel (Jesus' identity and actions) to the *consequences* of the gospel (salvation for those who believe). When this happens, we might start to see salvation as the result of "having the right beliefs about Jesus" rather than the result of who Jesus is and what he has done. In reality, the gospel is not about what *we* do but what *Christ* has done for us. His actions demand a response of faith from us, but it is not our response that saves us, but Christ himself.

What must we do to be saved?

The answer is simple: "Believe on the Lord Jesus, and you will be saved" (Acts 16:31). To believe is to have *faith*, and salvation comes "through faith in Christ Jesus" (2 Timothy 3:15). Faith involves our assent to the claims underlying the gospel, particularly the claims about who Christ is and what he has done for our salvation. Since this assent involves a "conviction of things not seen" (Hebrews 11:1), it takes the form of *trust*. The Holy Spirit enables us to trust God by supplying us with God's own wisdom so that we "may understand the gifts bestowed on us by God" and trust in Christ even if we do not yet fully comprehend who he is and what he has done (1 Corinthians 2:12-13). This kind of trust involves our hearts, emotions and actions as well as our minds. Faith is not simply believing things *about* Jesus but believing *in* Jesus by trusting that he truly is "the way and the truth and the life" (John 14:6) and committing to "walk just as he walked" as his disciple (1 John 2:6). In this sense, faith is an ongoing total commitment to Christ rather than a one-time intellectual decision about him.

What does it mean to have faith in Christ?

We can summarize the concept of faith in three points. First, since faith involves belief in the gospel about Jesus, we have faith when we actually *hear and respond* to the gospel. Or, as Paul puts it: "faith comes from what

is heard, and what is heard comes through the word of Christ" (Romans
10:17). This helps explain why, after Jesus' death and resurrection, the
apostles immediately traveled around the world to share the gospel with
everyone who would listen. "How are they to believe in one of whom
they have never heard?" Paul asks (Romans 10:14). Of course, this idea
raises difficult questions, especially when we consider the cases of infant
children or those who are mentally incapacitated. In these instances, the
church traditionally has found comfort in the goodness and justice of
God, while also emphasizing that these exceptions do not in any way
undermine the reality that the proclamation of the gospel to nonbelievers
is the central mission of the church.

Second, the fact that faith is an ongoing commitment to Christ means
that faith and salvation are linked to our *repentance*. To repent is to recognize one's sin, confess it to God and abandon it to pursue a life of
obedience. Repentance reorients our lives: we once were headed toward
death, but now we are headed toward eternal life with God. This new
path affects our self-identity and the way we live on a daily basis. "You
also must consider yourselves dead to sin and alive to God in Christ
Jesus," Paul says. "Therefore, do not let sin exercise dominion in your
mortal bodies" (Romans 6:11-12). Our new life in Christ prompts us to
grow into the reality of who we are because of our relationship to him.
This growth is constant, and it means that our repentance is not a one-
time event but an ongoing posture marked by our act of "forgetting what
lies behind and straining forward to what lies ahead" (Philippians 3:13).
We do both of these things through the Spirit, who guides and empowers
us along the way (Galatians 5:25).

Third, the centrality of faith helps us place our *actions* in the right
perspective. Christians clearly are commanded to do good deeds in the
pattern of Christ and his apostles. "Keep on doing the things that you
have learned and received and heard and seen in me," Paul says, "and the
God of peace will be with you" (Philippians 4:9). Among other things,
these actions involve growing in the knowledge of God, following after
Christ in obedience and displaying the fruit of the Spirit in our lives. Yet
as we do these things, we know that they are the result of our salvation
rather than the source of it. Our virtuous actions stem from God's work

in and through us, so we can never take credit for them: "this is not your own doing; it is the gift of God—not the result of works, so that no one may boast" (Ephesians 2:8-9). God is the sole source of both our salvation *and* its consequences in our lives.

> **Predestination and Election.** *Predestination* and *election* are closely related terms that describe the relationship between God's eternal being and divine will and our salvation through Christ and the Spirit within human history. Predestination has a wider range of reference, as it is used to refer to God's sovereign determination over all events in line with his divine wisdom and nature. Election is used more specifically to refer to God's decision and plan about our salvation. Taken together, these doctrines emphasize that our salvation by God through Jesus Christ and the Holy Spirit is not an accidental or haphazard event but the result of God's specific plan, since God "accomplishes all things according to his counsel and will" (Ephesians 1:11). Both of these terms have been the subject of intense debate throughout Christian history, especially with respect to the question of how our human freedom and will relates to God's divine plan.

What role does the Holy Spirit play in salvation?

God gave humans life when he created them, but with their fall into sin, humans chose to embrace death instead. This choice is reflected in each one of us, both in our darkened minds and our failure to honor God with our actions (Romans 1:21). Our salvation by God includes the gift of a "new spirit" who renews our minds and enables us to live in obedience once again.

God promises this gift in the Old Testament when, faced with Israel's repeated disobedience to the law, God tells the Israelites that he will enable them to follow the law by giving them his own Spirit: "I will put my spirit within you, and make you follow my statutes and be careful to observe my ordinances" (Ezekiel 36:27). With the arrival of Jesus, John the Baptist announces that this promise has been fulfilled, because Jesus is the one who "will baptize you with the Holy Spirit and fire" (Luke 3:16). Jesus claims this promise for himself by saying that he would ask his Father to send his disciples the "Spirit of truth," who would come to dwell within them (John 14:16-17). He fulfills the promise after his resurrection, when he tells his disciples, "I am sending upon you what my Father promised; so stay here in the city until you have been clothed with power from on high" (Luke 24:49). This power arrives at Pentecost when all the believers are "filled with the Holy Spirit" (Acts 2:4). Shortly thereafter, when Peter preaches the gospel for the first time, he includes the gift of the Spirit in his description of what salvation involves: "Repent, and be baptized every one of you in the name of Jesus Christ so that your sins may be forgiven; and you will receive the gift of the Holy Spirit. For the promise is for you, for your children, and for all who are far away, everyone whom the Lord our God calls to him" (Acts 2:38-39).

Peter's sermon helps us see that, whenever we talk about salvation, we should refer to both the victory over sin and death that Jesus Christ won on the cross *and* the new life that comes to us through the gift of the Holy Spirit. Salvation is a *trinitarian* event. Paul provides a helpful example in this regard throughout his letters. He proclaims "Christ crucified," but he also makes sure to say that this proclamation is a "demonstration of the Spirit and of power" (1 Corinthians 2:4; see also 1:24). He explains that faith comes as a gift of the Spirit, because "no one can say, 'Jesus is Lord!' except by the Holy Spirit" (1 Corinthians 12:3). He also says that the Spirit serves as a "seal" of our salvation (Eph 1:13; 4:30), which is a reference to the ancient system of placing a wax or clay seal on something to signify ownership or authenticity. His point is that God's gift of the Spirit gives us confidence that the God "who began a good work among [us] will bring it to completion" (Philippians 1:6). We can have this confidence even in the face of death, because we know that the one "who raised Christ from the dead will give life to [our] mortal bodies also through his Spirit that dwells in [us]" (Romans 8:11). The Spirit serves as a "pledge of our inheritance toward redemption" (Ephesians 1:14), and he helps us anticipate our future redemption by transforming our minds

(Romans 8:5), producing the fruit of the Spirit in our lives (Galatians 5:16-25) and enabling us to use the gifts God has given us to build up and serve the church (1 Corinthians 12:7-10). For all these reasons, the work of Christ and the Holy Spirit for our salvation are intimately linked, so that we cannot talk about the one without the other.

How does Jesus' crucifixion save us from sin and death?

This question relates to the doctrine of the atonement, which explains how Christ's death on the cross reconciles sinful humans to God. The key is to start with the personal nature of our sin, God's wrath against it and our need for repentance and forgiveness. The New Testament often describes our situation in legal terms: every human stands guilty of sin before God and faces the "day of wrath, when God's righteous judgment will be revealed" (Romans 2:5). However, the good news is that "while we still were sinners Christ died for us," taking the consequences of our sin upon himself so that "we will be saved through him from the wrath of God" (Rom 5:8-9). "For our sake," Paul says, "he made him to be sin who knew no sin, so that in him we might become the righteousness of God" (2 Corinthians 5:21).

Jesus Christ's death on the cross saves us because Christ stands in our place as our substitute: he takes our sin and God's wrath against it as if they were his own so that we might be free from them and stand in right relationship with God. In this way, Christ's substutionary death for us becomes the path to our righteousness and eternal life.

But how does this substitution actually *work*?

The best way to explain how Christ's death on the cross saves us is to look at the way the New Testament writers draw upon the sacrificial ceremonies of Israel to explain and interpret it. We find the details of one such ceremony in Leviticus 16. God had made himself available to Israel by residing in the tabernacle, which held the ark of the covenant upon which was the mercy seat. He commanded Aaron the priest to bring a bull and two goats to the tabernacle to offer a sacrifice of atonement for Israel's sins. He instructed Aaron to sacrifice the bull for his sins and those of his family, one goat for the sins of Israel, and then sprinkle the blood of both in front of the mercy seat. The symbolism is clear: Aaron's act of placing the blood of the sacrifices between God and himself indicates that the bull and the goat were substitutes for Aaron and the people, because they had received the judgment for Israel's sin in Israel's place. After Aaron had made this offering, God then commanded him to bring the remaining goat before the altar and place his hands upon it while confessing Israel's sins. This action marked the transfer of the iniquities to the goat, who was then released into the wilderness, taking Israel's sins away. The result was forgiveness: "from all your sins you shall be clean before the LORD" (Leviticus 16:30).

These are the kinds of images Paul has in mind when he says that God put Christ forth as a "sacrifice of atonement by his blood" and that God "passed over the sins previously committed" (Romans 3:25). The difference between those earlier offerings and Christ's sacrifice is that Christ's death is sufficient for every sin for all time. This is the point the author of Hebrews makes when he argues that Christ "entered once for all into the holy places, not by means of the blood of goats and calves but by means of his own blood, thus securing an eternal redemption" (Hebrews 9:12 ESV). His substitution for us means that even though we are sinners, we can "have confidence to enter the holy places by the blood of Jesus" (Hebrews 10:19 ESV). By taking our sin and God's wrath against it upon himself, Christ frees us from their burden and restores our relationship with God. Peter summarizes it well: Christ "bore our sins in his body on the cross, so that, free from sins, we might live for righteousness; by his wounds you have been healed" (1 Peter 2:24).

What are the implications of Christ's atoning death for our daily lives?

From the starting point of substitution, several implications of Christ's atoning work can be brought forth to help us understand the difference it makes in our daily life. For example, the New Testament often describes Christ's saving work in terms of God's conflict with the principalities and powers who stand against humanity (1 Corinthians 2:6; Ephesians 1:21). Through Christ's death, God has "rescued us from the power of darkness and transferred us into the kingdom of his beloved Son" (Colossians 1:13). So, even in the storms of life, we rest in the confidence that God has "disarmed the rulers and authorities" by taking our sin and punishment in our place (Colossians 2:15). Christ's substitutionary death also frees us from the burden of our individual sin. Jesus uses this imagery when he says that he has come "to give his life as a ransom for many" (Mark 10:45), and Paul does as well when he notes that we were "bought with a price" (1 Corinthians 6:20). The implication is that Christ's death reconfigures our relationship with God by removing any debts we have incurred and opening the door to forgiveness. His death also carries ethical implications for us by providing us with an example to imitate as we attempt to "live in love, as Christ loved us and gave himself up for us, a fragrant offering and sacrifice to God" (Ephesians 5:2). We bear witness to Christ by living our lives in the pattern of the cross, "carrying in the body the death of Jesus, so that the life of Jesus may also be made visible in our bodies" (2 Corinthians 4:10). In this sense, Jesus' crucifixion is not simply a way for us to escape death; it shows us the path to true life.

But how can we be saved if we're still sinful?

Not only does Jesus Christ take our sin and the penalty for it upon himself, but he also makes it possible for us to exist in right relationship with God. The church's explanation for how this happens is found in its doctrine of justification, which is the doctrine that works out the implications of Jesus Christ's obedient life and sacrificial death for our salvation. As discussed in the previous question, even though Jesus always obeyed God's law and "committed no sin" (1 Peter 2:22), he took our sins and their penalty in our place by dying on the cross for us. This substitution leaves us with a "not guilty" verdict as we face God's judgment with respect to our sin. Yet being "not guilty" is not the same as being righteous. This is where Jesus' obedient life comes in. As our sin is debited to his account, Christ's active righteousness is credited to our account. Through this exchange, we are "made righteous" (Romans 5:19). This fulfills God's promise that the Messiah of Israel would "make many righteous" as well as "bear their iniquities" (Isaiah 53:11), and it marks our justification before God. The fact that we did nothing to deserve or earn this justification means that it comes to us as gift of God's grace. And since God gives this gift to "all who believe" (Romans 3:22), our justification is by *grace* through *faith*.

Since our justification comes by faith rather than though our works, it happens instantaneously rather than gradually, taking the form of an immediate declaration of innocence. This helps explain why we are able to stand righteous before God while also remaining sinners through and through. The fact that God declares us righteous even though we simultaneously remain sinful does not make our standing before God counterfeit, but rather, it emphasizes how closely our salvation is linked to Christ himself. The righteousness that we have before God is *Christ's* righteousness rather than our own, and we have it only because we are in union with him. This idea is expressed throughout the New Testament

Adoption. The metaphor of *adoption* provides a helpful way to think about salvation, because it captures both the relational and the legal aspects of our new status in Christ. Just as an adopted child receives a new and intimate relationship with the adoptive family, believers relate to God intimately and without fear, as a child relates to a father (Romans 8:15). We share in the full benefits of family membership, including the right to an inheritance: "you are no longer a slave but a child, and if a child then also an heir, through God" (Galatians 4:7). And this new status and inheritance comes with responsibilities, because our adoption into God's family means that we should begin to resemble this family. In our case, this looks like being "conformed to the image of [God's] Son, in order that he might be firstborn within a large family" (Romans 8:29).

by the phrases "in Christ" or "in him" (see, for example, Ephesians 1:3-14). These phrases indicate that our own existence can no longer be defined apart from what Christ has done for us and how he relates to us in and through his Spirit. "I have been crucified with Christ," Paul says, "and it is no longer I who live, but it is Christ who lives in me. And the life I now live in the flesh I live by faith in the Son of God, who loved me and gave himself for me" (Galatians 2:19-20).

What difference does God's justification of us make for how we live?

Our justification by Christ carries implications for how we act, because it is impossible to be in union with Christ without also becoming *like* Christ. Paul talks about this as the process of taking off the "old self" and putting on the "new self" (Colossians 3:9-10; Ephesians 4:22-25). It is clear, however, that the good works that result from this transformation are the *product* of our union with Christ rather than the means of it. Paul summarizes it well: he stands righteous before God only because he can be "found in him, not having a righteousness of my own that comes from the law, but that which is through faith in Christ—the righteousness that comes from God on the basis of faith" (Philippians 3:9 NIV).

One of the great benefits of God's justification of us by grace through faith is *confidence*: since our righteousness comes from Christ rather than ourselves, we can be sure that our standing before God is secure. "There is now no condemnation for those who are in Christ Jesus" (Romans 8:1 NIV). Our justification in Christ also provides motivation for our task to share the gospel with nonbelievers. Since we no longer have to work for our own benefit in order to secure our own salvation, we are free to work for the benefit of others by making sure they have heard the good news. In this sense, justification by grace through faith is the fuel for the mission of the church. It also puts our Christian life in perspective. As fallen sinners, we will often fail and disappoint when the storms of life come our way. Yet we do not proclaim good news that focuses on who we are or what we do, but on who *Christ* is and what he has done for us.

Where does the resurrection fit into our salvation?

If a human is both soul *and* body, then the salvation of a human must involve the body as well as the soul. The ultimate salvation of our bodies will happen in the final resurrection when God will raise them from their graves. This is part of God's final victory over death (1 Corinthians 15:26).

Our resurrection will follow the pattern of Christ's resurrection, which Paul calls the "first fruits" of the more general resurrection to come (1 Corinthians 15:20). Christ's resurrection was *bodily*, as shown by the fact that he carried the scars of his crucifixion, ate food and could be physically touched (Luke 24:39-42; John 20:27). And yet his body also had remarkable properties, as demonstrated by his ability to appear suddenly in the middle of locked rooms (Luke 24:36; John 20:19). From these accounts, we can discern that our resurrected bodies will be physical like our current ones yet also transformed in some way. Paul discusses the nature of this transformation when he explains that Christians die with a "physical body" but will be raised with a "spiritual body" (1 Corinthians 15:44). It is important to pay attention to the original Greek terms here to avoid confusion. Paul is not drawing a contrast between a material body and a non-material body, as might seem to be the case from the English translation. The word behind "physical" is *psychikos*, which indicates a body that is powered by normal human *psyche* or soul. The word "spiritual" is *pneumatikos*, drawn from the root *pneuma* ("spirit"), which Paul uses here refer to a body powered by God's own Spirit. His point is that the power that animates our resurrected bodies will be different from the power that animates our current bodies. While our current bodies live by the power of our own human souls and thus are liable to sin and death, our resurrected bodies will live by the power of the Holy Spirit and so will not fall prey to sin or death.

This distinction helps explain what Paul means when he says that "flesh and blood cannot inherit the kingdom of God, nor does the perishable inherit the imperishable" (1 Corinthians 15:50). He is not saying that our resurrected bodies will be "ghost-like," but rather, his point is that our bodies will be given unique properties enabling us to live in eternal fellowship with God. Even though Paul admits that the nature of this transformation remains a "mystery" to him (1 Corinthians 15:51), he remains fully confident that our resurrection will be like Christ's own resurrection: "we will certainly be united with him in a resurrection like his" (Romans 6:5). This insight, as well as Paul's claims about the Spirit's role in our resurrection, helps us to understand the importance of his claim that "you will reap eternal life from the Spirit" (Galatians 6:8). Our eternal life in our resurrected bodies will be a *transformed* life, because we will live always and at every moment through the power of the Holy Spirit and the mediation of Christ—all to the glory of God the Father.

What difference does our future resurrection make for our lives in the present?

As Christians, we live in anticipation of our resurrected life to come by committing to "walk not according to the flesh but according to the Spirit" (Romans 8:4). This fits with God's Old Testament promises about the Holy Spirit, and it reinforces why we can never take credit for or boast about our works. At the same time, Paul points to the resurrection as the reason why we should be "excelling in the work of the Lord" and why we can know that our "labor is not in vain" (1 Corinthians 15:58). The fact that our bodies will be raised from the dead shows that our pursuit of holiness in our bodies *matters*. It does not matter for our standing before God, since Christ secured our relationship with God on our

Legalism and Antinomianism. The doctrine of justification helps us avoid the errors of legalism and antinomianism (or, lawlessness). We fall into *legalism* when we think our relationship with God depends upon our obedience to God's law. *Antinomianism* is the mistake of thinking that God's grace abolishes God's law by rendering its standards irrelevant. These errors mirror one another, because they both stem from a faulty view of salvation. God does not abandon his moral standards when he saves us, but rather, he changes our relationship to these standards by freeing us from guilt through Christ and by empowering us to obedience through the Spirit. Through Christ and the Spirit, we have both a clear sense of God's holiness as well as the confidence that God himself will enable us to reflect his holiness the way we live our lives without fear of condemnation when we fail. The end result is "faith working through love" (Galatians 5:6).

behalf through his own body. Rather, our actions matter because they bear testimony to what God has done, offering an embodied witness of praise and gratitude to God. Indeed, the scars on Jesus' resurrected body will forever glorify God as they testify to his victory over sin and death. His example prompts us to examine our own lives in light of the pattern of his life, so that when we dwell with God in the new heavens and new earth (Revelation 21:1-27), the marks on our resurrected bodies will bear testimony to what God has done for our salvation.

8

WHO IS THE HOLY SPIRIT?

Jeffrey W. Barbeau

Imaginative visions of divine spirit fill our culture in literature, music, television and film. In George Lucas's *Star Wars*, characters are drawn to good or evil by the Force. Darth Vader, Luke Skywalker, and many other characters square off in a cosmic battle of good versus evil by using—or misusing—a power that pervades the entire universe. More recently, in James Cameron's international sensation *Avatar* (2009), a similar spiritual power connects all living things. Plants, animals and other creatures form a living eco-system permeated by a single, spiritual force.

Surrounded by such diverse images, Christians face two extremes. Some live in a state of "fear of the Spirit" or *pneumatophobia*. Some say that an intellectual study of the Holy Spirit is tantamount to attempting to capture the wind. In order to avoid falling prey to emotionalism, these Christians would rather ignore the question altogether or limit the conversation to the sparse and sometimes confusing language of Christian creeds. By contrast, other Christians prefer the very "obsession with the Spirit" that others fear, living in a state of *pneumatomania*. These believers speak about the Holy Spirit constantly and link almost every happy occurrence to a supernatural encounter with God. Most do not handle snakes or drink poisonous strychnine (though some, erroneously interpreting Mark 16:17–18, have regrettably tried just that), but they act as if their every wish can and will be fulfilled by the power of the Spirit. The rigorous demands of these Christians can make other believers feel that if they haven't had a unique and powerful encounter with the Holy Spirit, they may well not be Christians at all! With *pneumatophobia* and *pneumatomania* present at every turn, the need for a clearly articulated pneumatology, or study of the doctrine of the Holy Spirit, is crucial.

In fact, many Christians aren't even sure about the form of the question! Is the Spirit a "who" or a "what"? Historically, Christians have maintained that the Spirit is, above all, a "who." While I could certainly ask about a student in my classroom "What is Tim?," it would be more typical to ask others "Who is Tim?" The first question is certainly logical, since Tim is a human being and a student, among other things. But in the context of a classroom I would ask others "who" Tim is because they have a relationship with him: they know him, care about his welfare and relate to him as fellow learners in the community. Similarly, Christians may ask "What is the Spirit?" and rightly explain that the Spirit names the immaterial, divine presence in the world. But, in the context of the church, Christians ask "Who is the Spirit?" because we believe that the Spirit relates to creation through direct, personal actions. The apostle Paul, for example, repeatedly refers to the Spirit's personal agency by using active verbs such as "helps" (Romans 8:26), "intercedes" (Romans 8:27), "searches" (1 Corinthians 2:10), teaches (1 Corinthians 2:13), "calls out" (Galatians 4:6) and "dwells" (2 Timothy 1:14 ESV). These specific acts indicate that the Holy Spirit is not an impersonal life-force or power, but God's personal and active presence in the world.

The Bible identifies the Spirit by several names, including "Spirit of God," "Holy Spirit" and "Spirit of Christ." Reference to the Spirit as the "Spirit of God" can be found throughout the Bible, but one especially prominent theme is that of creation and new creation. The Spirit of God is present from the beginning of the creation account in Genesis (Genesis 1:2) and at the center of the life-giving acts of creation (Genesis 2:7), as well. Paul also describes our knowledge of God's redemptive work as one that depends upon the Spirit of God: "no one knows the thoughts of God except the Spirit of God" (1 Corinthians 2:11). By the Spirit of God, we understand God's ways and embrace what we would otherwise regard as foolishness. Just as the Spirit of God brought original life to creation, so, too, new life emerges by the re-creative or regenerative work of the Spirit of God.

The name "Holy Spirit" teaches us about both God and humans. While God the Father, Son, and Spirit are all "holy" (that is, "sacred" or "set apart"), the designation of the Spirit as the "Holy Spirit" reminds us that the Spirit *is* true holiness and the Spirit is the true source of *our* holiness. We are made new by a work of God and continue to grow in likeness to God by the Holy Spirit. When the Psalmist declares, "Do not cast me from your presence or take your Holy Spirit from me" (Psalm 51:11), he speaks of God's unique work of consecration.

Finally, the Bible refers to the Spirit as the "Spirit of Christ." When Jesus spoke to the disciples, he specifically promised that the Father would send the Spirit in his name and on his behalf: "But the Advocate, the Holy Spirit, whom the Father will send in my name, will teach you all things and will remind you of everything I have said to you" (John 14:26). Notably, John does not indicate that the Spirit *is* Christ. The two names are not interchangeable masks of a divine deception (consider the baptism of Jesus, where Father, Son and Spirit are all present without confusion). Rather, the Spirit of Christ is synonymous with the Spirit of God: "You, however, are not in the realm of the flesh but are in the realm of the Spirit, if indeed the Spirit of God lives in you. And if anyone does not have the Spirit of Christ, they do not belong to Christ" (Romans 8:9). For this reason, Christians affirm that whatever we say about the Spirit should reflect the one in whose name the Spirit has been sent: Jesus Christ.

Why all the recent attention to the Holy Spirit?

There are many reasons that Christian pastors and theologians are talking about the Spirit more than ever before in the history of Christianity. Above all, the changing landscape of Christianity around the world has shaped our theological conversations. Pentecostal and charismatic churches, especially from the majority world, account for a significant part of the growth of Christianity in the last one hundred years. Scholars estimate that the movement currently accounts for over 614,000,000 Christians worldwide, with more than 36,000 new members added through these churches every day. Far from being a religion in decline, Christianity is growing globally and a major reason is because of churches that give witness to the powerful work of the Spirit of God among them. In fact, some scholars predict that the variety of "charismatic" Christians will comprise the majority of Christians worldwide by the year 2050.

These recent "signs of the times" could easily mislead us into the belief that the Spirit was only at work among the apostles and today. In fact, the testimony of history provides fascinating examples of Christians in every generation who believed that the Spirit of God was at work powerfully among them. From monks to mystics, revolutionaries to evangelists, Christians across denominational boundaries in century after century have recognized that the Spirit works among God's people.

The Spirit and Global Pentecostalism. The results of a recent survey conducted by The Pew Forum on Religion and Public Life (2006) provide a snapshot of how Christians worldwide associate the active presence of the Holy Spirit with divine healings, miracles and adherence to traditional Christian doctrines.[1] For example, the survey reveals that many Christians who identify as Pentecostal believe that they have personally experienced or observed a divine healing. In most regions of the world, too, a majority of Pentecostals report experiencing personal divine revelations and witnessing some form of demonic exorcism. Similarly, Pentecostals worldwide typically have higher rates of belief in the authority of the Bible, the possibility of miracles today and adherence to traditional moral values than other Christians located in the same geographic region. If Pentecostalism continues to outpace other varieties of Christian belief and practice in the coming decades, what do these characteristics indicate about the importance of pneumatology in the future global theological conversation?

Where was the Spirit before Pentecost?

Pentecost marks the emergence of God's new community, a people set apart by the Spirit for renewed life and mission (Acts 2). But while Christians rightly associate the outpouring of God's Spirit with the Pentecost event, the Spirit of God is clearly active throughout the history of creation. The Spirit of God is present in the Genesis account of creation, indicating that the earth is the temple of God's presence. The *ruah*

(Hebrew for "spirit," "breath") gives life or vitality to humans and, even after the fall, continues to be present with God's people (Genesis 2:7; Job 33:4; Psalm 104:29-30). Individually, the Spirit's presence is found among those who serve God, as with the judges of Israel such as Gideon, Jephthah and Samson (Judges 6; 11; 13). The people of Israel, moreover, knew that God's presence was with them corporately in the tabernacle and temple (Exodus 40:34-35; 1 Kings 8:10-11). The prophets spoke of God's promise to Israel, too, noting that God's Spirit would be in them in the restoration (Ezekiel 36:26-27) as well as in the Messiah, the one who would deliver them (Isaiah 11; 42; 61). Thus, when the New Testament writers identified Jesus as the Christ, the anointed one, it is fitting that they associated the presence of the Spirit with him at his incarnation (Matthew 1:18), baptism (Mark 1:10), temptation (Luke 4:1) and resurrection (Romans 8:11). In fact, around the commencement of Jesus' public ministry, he took up the Isaiah scroll and associated its words of liberation with himself: "The Spirit of the Lord is on me, because he has anointed me to proclaim good news to the poor . . ." (Luke 4:18 ESV). So, long before Pentecost, the Spirit of God actively worked among God's people and even identified the one who would set the people free.

Why does the Bible use so many symbols for the Spirit?

Examples of God's presence, which Christians typically associate with the Holy Spirit, can be found throughout the Old and New Testaments alike. Biblical writers often use material objects to describe the presence of the Spirit of God in various events. The Bible refers to the presence of the Spirit in breath (Psalm 33:6), wind (Acts 2:2), fire (Acts 2:3), a cloud (Exodus 16:10), water (John 4:13-14) and a dove (John 1:32), among many others.

Since we often rely on material signs to know God, God reaches out to us in a manner that we can comprehend. In many cases, the biblical author indicates that the Spirit's presence is similar to some known, material object. At other times, the Spirit seems to have taken on material or embodied form in order to provide a concrete reminder of God's real presence among the people. In either case, God's self-revelation in these material forms reminds us that God accommodates to our finite understanding. Appearances of the Spirit in material form remind us that

God's presence can be known in the concrete forms of our existence and, more importantly, that God wishes to communicate himself to us in order to engage us in relationship. Our encounter with God is always spiritual *and* material. The Christian hope is not to get *out* of this world, but to know God more fully *in* this world, with all its frustrations, sorrows, joys and blessings.

But if the Spirit is "personal" rather than a cloud, fire or water, then what gender is the Spirit?

Above all, Christians believe that God is neither male nor female. The use of terms such as "heavenly Father" (Matthew 5:48) and "I am God's Son" (John 10:36) are analogies that help us to understand different types of relationships. God is not a father in the way that a human male is a father by acts of physical procreation. Rather, God relates to humans as a parent who cares for a child; the relationship of Jesus to the Father is one of harmony amidst difference. In fact, although it is the case that the Word of God is incarnate in Jesus Christ, as Christians we refuse the claim that Jesus' maleness in any way privileges all men any more than his eye color or height might privilege certain types of humans over others. What changed all history is that God took on our humanity.

So, in light of these reminders, what pronoun(s) should Christians use for the Holy Spirit? Scripture doesn't provide a single answer and biblical scholars are rightly cautious when assigning gender based on linguistic forms. The Hebrew word *ruah* is usually feminine, but the idea of the Spirit's personal agency isn't clearly developed in the Old Testament either. Some have suggested that if the New Testament writers had used Hebrew, they may very well have employed the feminine *ruah* in their writings and this would have been passed down to us through feminine pronouns (*she*). However, New Testament writers used the Greek word for spirit or *pneuma*, which is neuter (*it*). English, too, has a neuter form for spirit, so *it* has become a part of common English usage. In fact, the English use of the neuter pronoun likely contributes to confusion about "who" or "what" the Spirit is in the first place!

What about masculine forms (*he*)? In the New Testament, the Gospel of John refers to the Spirit as "Counselor" or "Helper" from *parakletos*

(John 14:26; 15:26), which takes the masculine form. Interestingly, in Latin, *spirit* is masculine, too, and Latin forms have encouraged the general tendency in English to use *he* whenever no clear gender is assigned.

But if God is without gender and the language we use is analogous, how should we refer to the Spirit of God? Some Christians strongly advocate that we should make a point of correcting the widespread misuse of the masculine for God by asserting the corrective *she*. Indeed, the misuse of gender forms has harmed women so often that there is a good case for linguistic protest as a path toward right thinking and practice. Perhaps *she* also captures aspects of God's nature more effectively than stereotypically masculine connotations for God (consider the dynamic portrait of God in William Young's *The Shack* for some sense of the risks and rewards of such departures). Other Christians believe that we ought to continue with masculine or neuter pronouns for the Spirit because those are the forms that we have inherited in English. They argue that departing from common practice unnecessarily causes conflict and confusion. However, persisting in unreflective traditions carries other risks, not least in compounding problems through the potentially depersonalizing use of the neuter form *it*.

Any of the three forms are permissible, whether he, it, or she. However, we do best to avoid gendering the Spirit of God at all. While it is sometimes necessary and certainly appropriate to use gendered pronouns in reference to God, we should avoid perpetuating the notion that the Godhead is composed of male and female parts. Instead, we need to encourage a wider recognition of the Spirit's personal presence and agency.

Should we pray to the Holy Spirit?

Yes and no. Since Christians believe in one God (Deuteronomy 6:4), our prayers to God are already implicitly addressed to the Holy Spirit. Prayer to God or members of the triune God is always implicitly or explicitly prayer addressed to the Father, Son and Holy Spirit together. Over and over again, we find that the works of God are not exclusive (as if Christians worship three gods), but always the work of the three persons of the Trinity in unity. If I imagine offering prayers to the Spirit exclusive of the Father or the Son, then I direct my prayers in vain. In fact, prayers offered to any member of the Trinity completely independent of the others are prayers offered to a false god, since Christians believe that God is one eternal being in three divine persons.

Therefore, Christians may direct prayers to the Holy Spirit, just as they may direct prayers to the Father or the Son. When we direct prayers to the Spirit specifically, we address God personally present and active in this world. On the basis of the Spirit of God, we are able to cry out and know that God hears our prayers. The Spirit helps us to pray and responds by providing inward assurance "that we are God's children" (Romans 8:16). So, when we sing out prayers such as "Spirit of the living God, fall afresh on me," we are rightly asking the Spirit of Christ to renew us again and again.

The Spirit and the Nicene Creed. Controversy over the doctrine of the Holy Spirit divided the churches of the East and West in what is now called the "Great Schism" of A.D. 1054. The schism was actually the culmination of a series of political and ecclesial disputes over the course of many centuries, but at least part of this enduring break involved the unilateral introduction of the phrase "of the Son" (*filioque* in Latin) to the Nicene Creed in the West. The creed in the West now reads, "We believe in the Holy Spirit, the Lord, the giver of life, who proceeds from the Father *and the Son*, who with the Father and the Son is worshiped and glorified, who has spoken through the prophets." While the West felt the addition clarified the relationship between the Son and Spirit, many bishops in the East worried that the addition not only signaled a dramatic abuse of authority (in changing the words of a universal creed), but also risked subordinating the eternal Spirit to the authority of the Son.

Was Jesus "filled" with the Spirit?

Yes . . . but not because he lacked anything. Jesus is fully human and fully divine in one undivided person. Since Jesus is fully God, he lacked nothing at all (this historical Christian belief is often called "Logos Christology").

Yet Old Testament promises about the Messiah, the anointed one, are very clear that the Spirit would be his distinguishing "mark" (sometimes connected to a theological position known as "Spirit Christology"). The problem with affirming that Jesus is the Word (Logos Christology) apart from the presence of the Spirit (Spirit Christology), however, is to risk ignoring the Old Testament promises, denying the inner union of God and stripping away the basis of our own inheritance as the children of God.

Although the Spirit is actively involved in every aspect of Jesus' life and ministry, his baptism in the Jordan River provides the paradigm for Christian salvation. Matthew describes the event as follows: "As soon as Jesus was baptized, he went up out of the water. At that moment heaven was opened, and he saw the Spirit of God descending like a dove and alighting on him. And a voice from heaven said, 'This is my Son, whom I love; with him I am well pleased'" (Matthew 3:16-17). What happened here? Some say that God took Jesus as his Son in that very moment. This belief was common in some fringe circles of the early church (the belief became known as "adoptionism") and rejected for failing to account for his eternal being as well as the events surrounding his unique birth. Others claim that nothing happened at the baptism. The event only marks a moment of preparation for Jesus' public ministry in which he was set apart publicly for a ministry of preaching and teaching.

The baptism of Jesus was neither an instance of divine "adoption" nor divine "public relations." To understand what happened, we must look to the biblical account of salvation. Paul describes our justification in Christ as being "marked in him with a seal, the promised Holy Spirit" (Ephesians 1:13). While Jesus did not need salvation as with all those who are subject to original sin, his participation in baptism does show us the way of regeneration. The voice from heaven declaring Christ as God's Son thereby typifies divine acceptance for all who follow in the way of Christ. Moreover, Jesus demonstrated the manner in which the Father declares those who believe to be acceptable, sets them on the path to a completely holy and loving life and empowers them for active service in this world. The baptism in water and the Spirit that Jesus received was the anointing of his full humanity and the symbol of God's promise for all who believe in Christ.

How do I know that I have the Spirit?

The good news is that God promises that the Spirit will be with his people both individually and corporately. In 1 John, this promise is clearly proclaimed: "This is how we know that we live in him and he in us: He has given us of his Spirit. . . . If anyone acknowledges that Jesus is the Son of God, God lives in them and they in God" (1 John 4:13–15). One result of justification is the confidence that we now live Spirit-filled lives. To be "born again" is to receive new life by the Spirit of Christ (John 3). When does this happen? Just as Jesus' baptism brought confirmation of the work of the Spirit, so, too, our baptism in water signifies the time when God's Spirit symbolically marks us and formally indicates our entrance into the community of faith.

The Spirit also confirms these external promises through an inward knowing. Paul explains that the Spirit "testifies with our spirit that we are God's children" (Romans 8:16). This intuitive knowledge or "witness of the Spirit" brings confidence, comfort and peace to those who live the life of faith in Christ.

Of course, sometimes we believe lies about ourselves. On the one hand, we may not believe we are loved by God and must learn to trust God's promises against self-doubt. Alternately, however, we may imagine we are filled with the Holy Spirit, but our actions consistently challenge the claim. Again, 1 John offers guidance: "Whoever lives in love lives in God, and God in them. This is how love is made complete among us so that we will have confidence on the day of judgment: In this world we are like Jesus . . . . Whoever claims to love God yet hates a brother or sister is a liar" (1 John 4:16-17, 20). In other words, if we genuinely love God and neighbor, then our actions testify to the work of the Spirit of God in our lives. In fact, Paul uses the image of a fruitful tree in Galatians for just this reason. A healthy tree will bear fruit: the fruit of the Spirit (Galatians 5:22-23). While the term may sound rather cliché, Paul's analogy is actually quite profound. Our outward actions should reflect the presence of the Spirit of God in our lives, namely lives filled with "love, joy, peace, patience, kindness, goodness, faithfulness, gentleness and self-control."

Undoubtedly, scrutinizing every action and motivation for conformity to the Spirit can be exhausting. The good news is that, unlike a guilty conscience, the Spirit leads us to sincere repentance when we fall short and helps us to grow in likeness to God. While we might be tempted to think that patience or self-control is "not my fruit," God calls all Christians to grow in all the fruit of the Spirit. John Wesley called this movement towards total love of God and neighbor "going on to perfection."[2] Acknowledging God's promises, sensing the Spirit's inward witness and observing the fruit of the Spirit in our lives confirm that we are filled with the Holy Spirit.

What about the gifts of the Spirit?

Unlike the fruit of the Spirit, which are available to all, God gives different gifts of the Spirit to each of us. In fact, there are several different lists of spiritual gifts in the Bible. In Ephesians, the apostle distinguishes the work of apostles, prophets, evangelists, pastors and teachers as unique vocations within the churches (Ephesians 4:11). Writing to the Romans, Paul offers a list that partially overlaps the ministry gifts of Ephesians, but identifies them with something reminiscent of individual skills or talents: "We have different gifts, according to the grace given to each of us. If your gift is prophesying, then prophesy in accordance with your faith; if it is serving, then serve; if it is teaching, then teach" (Romans 12:6-8). 1 Corinthians 12–14 offers an expansive description of the use of gifts in the churches. Paul explains that members of the churches are given gifts for the good of the body, including words of wisdom and knowledge, faith, prophecy, tongues or the ability to interpret other tongues: "All these are the work of one and the same Spirit, and he distributes them to each one, just as he determines" (1 Corinthians 12:11). Notably, throughout much of Christian history, Christians have associated the gifts of the Spirit with words Isaiah spoke about the Messiah:

> The Spirit of the LORD will rest on him—
>> the Spirit of wisdom and of understanding,
>> the Spirit of counsel and of might,
>> the Spirit of the knowledge and fear of the LORD—
> and he will delight in the fear of the LORD. (Isaiah 11:2-3)

While Isaiah's list has a long history of acceptance, the emergence of Pentecostal and charismatic churches around the world teaching a "baptism in the Spirit" (conferred either with water baptism or subsequently) has tipped the balance toward the more spectacular gifts of *glossolalia* (speaking in other unknown languages), acts of healing, words of prophecy, and so forth.

Too often, though, Christians regard the gifts of the Spirit as badges of honor. Undoubtedly, there is something very impressive when an individual speaks words of wisdom to build up the body or works as a means of grace to bring healing to a wounded individual or community. We should remember, however, that Paul's most famous explication of love appears right in the middle of his discussion of the gifts in 1 Corinthians 12–14. Paul wanted the Christians to remember that the gifts of the Spirit without the fruit of the Spirit are dead: "If I speak in the tongues of men or of angels, but do not have love, I am only a resounding gong or a clanging cymbal" (1 Corinthians 13:1). Moreover, the gifts of the Spirit are given to all who have the Spirit of God. The words of the prophet in Joel 2:28-29 remind us of God's desire to work through all people:

> I will pour out my Spirit on all people.
> Your sons and daughters will prophesy,
>> your old men will dream dreams,
>> your young men will see visions.
> Even on my servants, both men and women,
>> I will pour out my Spirit in those days.

These words are a reminder that God's gift-giving is revolutionary. The Spirit challenges the prejudicial tendencies of this world. Not only young and old, but also men, women and servants will be filled with the Spirit, putting an end to the privileges of the powerful. In recognition of God's good gifts and the priority of love, then, we should neither timidly avoid nor selfishly demand the gifts of the Spirit, but earnestly seek and receive them for the well-being of the community of God.

Does the Holy Spirit work among non-Christians?

Yes. God is at work among all people. Christians believe that by God's prevening grace—the grace that precedes salvation—God reaches out to all people. John Wesley wrote that our God is the God of all people, "Yea, doubtless of the Mahometans [Muslims] and heathens also. His love is not confined."[3] So, while not all people respond to God's gracious stirring, God continues to be present and active among them.

I've heard that sin against the Holy Spirit is unforgivable. What is the sin against the Holy Spirit?

Matthew, Mark and Luke each mention the possibility of an "eternal" or "unforgivable" sin. In Mark, for example, Jesus states that "people can be forgiven all their sins and every slander they utter, but whoever blasphemes against the Holy Spirit will never be forgiven; they are guilty of an eternal sin" (Mark 3:28-29; compare Matthew 12:31-32 and Luke 12:10).

Charles Wesley on Divine Love

Come, Holy Ghost, our hearts inspire,
Let us Thine influence prove:
Source of the old prophetic fire,
Fountain of life and love.

Come, Holy Ghost, for moved by Thee
The prophets wrote and spoke;
Unlock the truth, Thyself the key,
Unseal the sacred book.

Expand Thy wings, celestial Dove,
Brood o'er our nature's night;
On our disordered spirits move,
And let there now be light.

God, through Himself, we then shall know
If Thou within us shine,
And sound with all Thy saints below,
The depths of love divine.

Charles Wesley (1707–1788), English hymn writer
and cofounder of Methodism[4]

These verses have caused many restless nights for Christians (and scholars!) through the centuries, but three notes are worth keeping in mind. First, the unforgivable sin appears to be the final denial of God. Since it is the Spirit of Christ who reaches out to us in our fallenness, it is resistance to God's gracious offer of reconciliation that is ultimately at stake. Second, while it is tempting to identify who may have committed such a sin, we do well to set our sights on God's gracious love and rest in his mercy. Finally, if this or any other sins in our lives continue to cause us worry, we can be certain that God remains present, calling us to renewal and cleansing by the Spirit.

WHO ARE HUMAN BEINGS?

David Lauber

As a Christian, I have to think carefully about how I define who I am. Is my identity tied up with the clothes I wear, the computer I use or the car I drive? Is my identity determined by how others perceive me? By how I perceive myself? Or, perhaps, by how God relates to me? Consider how often we attempt to secure our identity by attempting to impress others or by proving that we are important and deserve respect. Frequently, for example, when I am in a new social setting, I encounter the predicament of how to introduce myself. We are so often identified by what we do—by our jobs, titles and income. I have three standard ways of introducing myself. When I am being very honest and confident, I tell people that I am a teacher. And if they follow up, I say that I am a teacher of theology at a college. If, however, I am feeling the need to impress others, I say that I am college professor—to distinguish myself from other teachers. If I am really desperate, I inform others that I am a theologian—since this sounds so esoteric and impressive. So, we see that the question of individual identity is important and complicated. This comes out in how we view ourselves and how we project ourselves before others.

In his 2004 documentary *The Persuaders*, media and culture critic Douglas Rushkoff examines the unprecedented influence of advertising and marketing in contemporary American culture—from selling laundry detergent to electing the President of the United States.[1] Ruschkoff uncovers many startling elements of the persuasion industry, and in the course of doing so he describes how personal identity is understood in today's world.

One prominent theme of Rushkoff's work is the significance of brands and their role in accounting for individual personal identity. It turns out that we are not simply individuals who happen to use this brand or another; rather, our individual personal identity is actually shaped by the brands that we use. Long gone are the days when the job of advertising executives was to convince the public of the superiority of a product. According to advertising executive Douglas Atkins, the job of advertising in today's world is "to create and maintain a whole meaning system for people, through which they get identity and understanding of the world." As Rushkoff concludes, products are not fundamentally items that we purchase and use. Today they play a much greater role in our lives, as they "fill the empty places where non-commercial institutions, like schools and churches, might once have done the job. Brands become more than just a mark of quality, they become an invitation to a longed-for lifestyle, a ready-made identity."[2]

A clear example of this development is Apple computers. From 2006–2010 Apple ran a series of television ads in which one actor portrayed a Mac and another a PC. The aim of these commercials was not primarily to demonstrate the superiority of a Macintosh computer, as a computer. It was to sell an identity. The PC was nerdy and conventional—the standard company man. The Mac was hip and creative—the nonconformist individual. The question for the consumer is not, Do you use a Mac? The question is, Are you a Mac user? Are you a part of the Mac culture—part of the tribe?

Have our lives been reduced to lifestyle choices, and are our individual personal identities determined by what we buy? Are our contemporary lives so shallow that we rely upon brands to provide us with a "ready-made identity"? In a world dominated by the persuasion industry, individuals are either exceptionally free to find or create their identities from seemingly endless consumer choices, or they are unwitting sheep being manipulated again and again by global conglomerates who will do anything to make a profit. Either way, the message is that we are what we consume. We have traded a real life for a series of fleeting lifestyle choices. Consider how often these lifestyle choices, along with the labels of marketers, pigeonhole individuals as a type or instance of a particular demographic. We can imagine someone being labeled as a thirty-something, Mac-owning, libertarian, loft-dwelling urbanite, introvert, of Scandinavian descent, working in the tech industry, who drives a Subaru while drinking fair-trade coffee and listening to Arcade Fire.

Christian faith is fundamentally about personal identity (apart from what we own or what movement we attach ourselves to). The Bible tells the story of who we are in relation to God, the world and others. The study of theological anthropology takes up the specific issue of how human beings are in relation to God, and what difference this makes.

Do I have a soul, or am I just a body?

Typically we wonder what constitutes "personhood" and if a person has more than a body. For example, what would it mean to say that we also have a soul or spirit?

Often Christians uncritically embrace a Greek philosophical picture of the human person as an immortal soul that is housed within a finite and limited body—a body that is decaying and destined for destruction. Sometimes this is in response to contemporary scientific explanations of humanity that are materialist—we are fundamentally material bodies and nothing more. Consciousness is explained by brain chemistry and electrical signals. Often in response to these types of explanations, Christians insist on the existence of an immortal soul and this soul is given priority over the physical body.

This view, however, neglects the significance of physical, bodily existence, and ends up undermining the importance of a foundational Christian claim—the resurrection of the body. Instead, this dualist view considers material life on this earth as something to be endured until we put off the flesh, escape from our bodies and live as immortal souls in the presence of God.

The question that we must ask at this point is how does the Bible depict the human person? There are various terms used in the Old Testament to describe the human person. Terms such as: soul, spirit, heart and body. On first glance, and with certain presuppositions in mind, we might read these terms as designating different parts that together make up the human person. However, with further inspection we see that rather than describing discrete parts of the human person, these terms denote the whole human person from various angles. There is no basis in Hebrew Old Testament anthropology for a dualism between body and soul, or even a trichotomy of body, soul and spirit. The human creature is *a whole* person and cannot be divided into parts.

Things get a bit complicated when we turn to the New Testament, but the conclusion of a holistic vision of the human person remains the same. The complication is the result of the Hellenistic (Greek) setting of the New Testament writers, especially Paul. Paul uses terminology including *sarkikos* (fleshly), *psychikos* (physical or natural) and *pneumatikos* (spiritual) to describe the human person. He also speaks of salvation in terms of the renewal of the *nous* (mind) and the saving of the *pneuma* (spirit) through *gnosis* (knowledge) and *sophia* (wisdom). Furthermore, he employs the theme of warfare between the *sarx* (flesh) and the *pneuma* (spirit) and draws a distinction between the "outer self" and the "inner self" (Romans 8:1-17; 2 Corinthians 4:16).

Does this mean that Paul was influenced more by the dualistic Greek thought than by Old Testament anthropology? We must not jump to conclusions and read Paul as pitting the human soul or spirit, which is good, against the human flesh or body, which is inherently evil. Rather, we must see that Paul shares the outlook of the Old Testament, as he is concerned with the whole human person in relationship with God. And, Paul frames these convictions in light of the Hellenistic culture in which he lives.

When, for example, Paul speaks of the war between *sarx* (flesh) and *pneuma* (spirit), he is not suggesting that there is an "earthly" part of the person that is in conflict with a divine or spiritual part of the person. The problem that we face as human beings is not that we are *sarx* (fleshly). After all, the New Testament insists that Jesus, too, must be considered in terms of the flesh ("In the days of his flesh," Hebrews 5:7, and "The Word became flesh," John 1:14).[3] No, the problem is that in our current state our flesh is in bondage to sin, under the rule of sin (Romans 7:14; 8:3). Correspondingly, when Paul uses *pneuma* (spirit) it does not designate a particular aspect of the human person, the human spirit; rather, it designates the Holy Spirit, which is the essential source of life and power which comes from God, and from God alone. We are called, then, not to live according to our own human spirit. We are called to live in *the* Spirit—the Holy Spirit.

What difference does all of this make? We need to be very careful of concluding that the Bible endorses any type of ultimate dualism that pits an immortal and good soul against an inherently evil and dispensable material body. We are whole creatures, body and soul, and it is our entire self (body, mind, heart, soul and spirit) that must be ruled by the Holy Spirit and not by sin. And it is this entire and whole self that awaits the resurrection and life in the world to come.

So where do I find the image of God?

One of the most remarkable statements about humanity in Scripture is that human beings are created in the image of God (Genesis 1:26-27). This biblical affirmation is also one of the most mysterious and contested. This is a remarkable statement, because it tells us that although human beings are creatures among other creatures, human beings are unique. It is mysterious and contested, because there is no biblical and theological consensus regarding what exactly the image of God is. We must recognize the curious fact that in the Bible we have the affirmation *that* humans are created in the image of God, but we do not have clarity regarding *what* exactly the image of God is.

Theologians have tried to parse the meaning of the image of God with a variety of proposals. Perhaps humans are different because they possess rationality or creativity or imagination. Other theologians have pointed to activities that make us human. For example, we actively rule over the rest of creation. One current suggestion, which has gained support in a variety of theological circles, is to identify relationality as the image of God in humanity. This proposal stresses the relationality that is inherent in the trinitarian life of God—Father, Son and Holy Spirit—and claims that human beings mirror or image God as we live in relationship with others.

The difficulty with common proposals is that they all identify the image of God with a particular capacity or aspect of the human person. This suggests that we have the image of God as an individual possession, simply by virtue of our creation. I find this dissatisfying because it neglects a stress on the vital significance of human life lived in constant dependence on God's relation to us. Furthermore, I want to ask what we are to do with New Testament treatments of the image of God, especially the stress in that Jesus is the true image of God (Colossians 1:15; Hebrews 1:3; 2 Corinthians 4:4; Philippians 2:6). Our view of humanity and the image of God is altered when we focus on Christ instead of ourselves. When we focus on Christ as *the* true image of God and the manifestation of genuine humanity we see that we exhibit true humanity as we embrace the unique relationship we have with God—a relationship of holiness and righteousness (Ephesians 1:3-4; 4:22-24; Colossians 3:9-10) in which we glorify God in all that we do. In other words, the image of God is not something that we possess; rather, it is something that depends on our relationship with God. It is a calling to live in fellowship and communion with God.

Am I really free?

Few words resonate with our culture more strongly than "freedom." Everyone wants to be free. This freedom frequently takes the form of my individual freedom to be whoever I desire to be and to do whatever I want to do, so long as I do not infringe upon the freedom of others.

Given the bleak human history of oppression and coercion, there is something appropriate about affirming one's freedom from the dangerous power of external forces. However, when it comes to an understanding of human identity from the vantage point of Christian belief, the human assertion of autonomy is deeply flawed. It is flawed because it operates with the notion that individuals are free to construct their identities from scratch. Moreover, we are not only told to construct ourselves from nothing, we are encouraged to do this again and again. If we become dissatisfied with the identity we have constructed, we are told to try out something else. Think about how often we hear about the genius of certain entertainment stars who are constantly reinventing themselves, in an attempt to overcome the boredom and short attention span of the paying public.

The flaw of this notion of freedom is that it is far removed from the genuine Christian understanding of human identity as being a gift from God. According to Christian faith, I am not free to construct myself. Rather, Christian faith tells us that our identity, and with that our meaning, value and purpose, depends upon fitting ourselves within the world that God has made. We are creatures of a loving and gracious God, and it is by way of our communion with this God that we find our true identities.

The gospel of Jesus Christ is a gospel of freedom—"Where the Spirit of the Lord is, there is freedom" (2 Corinthians 3:17), and "For freedom Christ has set us free" (Galatians 5:1). The Christian understanding of freedom, however, differs dramatically from its philosophical and consumerist counterparts. Christian freedom is not essentially freedom *from* external demands and constraints so I can be whoever I choose and do whatever I want. Christian freedom is freedom *for* God, freedom *for* obedience to God's will. There is, of course, a liberating aspect of the gospel, as we are freed from bondage and enslavement to sin. Yet, this liberating aspect includes a new form of enslavement—we are no longer slaves to sin; we are now slaves to God, to righteousness (Romans 6:17-23). In short, God frees human beings so that they might live in obedience to his will, and it is in this obedience that human beings find their true identities and true freedom.

Some might protest that the notion of speaking of freedom in terms of obedience, self-denial and enslavement to God is contradictory and is, in fact, harmful to the individual. While Jesus' call to self-denial and obedience is challenging, it also comes with the promise that this is the way to abundant and true life—we find ourselves by losing ourselves and we experience abundant life as we live for the sake of God and others.

I like to compare the freedom of the Christian life with the freedom displayed by the finest of jazz improvisation. For example, in an improvisational performance a jazz pianist displays freedom and spontaneity. Yet, this extemporaneous performance is possible only because of a certain type of obedience—obedience to the standards of music theory, the execution of technique and years of dedicated practice. In fact, there is a direct correlation between the freedom a musician can exhibit in an improvisational performance and the cumulative amount of practice and experience this musician has. In a similar manner, a Christian life that is marked by freedom is a life that is ruled by discipline, practice and obedience.

What is our worst human failing?

Typically Christians claim that *pride* is our chief sin. We are arrogant and rebellious creatures, so the story goes, who challenge God's authority and desire to remove God from his position of power, replacing God with ourselves. Although there certainly is merit to this depiction of the strife that exists between humanity and God because of sin, I want to suggest that it is actually distrust and lack of faith that lie at the foundation of sinful human life.

When we look at the story of the tempter and Adam and Eve in Genesis 3, we see two prominent things. First, we see that the serpent's strategy was to raise questions in the mind of Eve, "Did God say . . . ?" (Genesis 3:1), and, after raising questions, the serpent asserts that God has in fact deceived Eve, "You will not die" (Genesis 3:4). The result of the serpent's tempting was to make Eve suspicious of God. She doubted whether God was telling her the truth. She doubted that God really had her and Adam's best interest in mind. It is her doubt and distrust that leads her to take the fruit and eat.

We see, second, that Adam and Eve ate from the tree of the knowledge of good and evil. This is significant because it shows that they refuse to live in dependent and trusting obedience to the command of God. They, instead, want to determine for themselves what is good and what is evil. They want to be independent and autonomous.

We were created with our true center in God. Our true center is not found within us but outside of us. So sin involves questioning God's desire for us. It involves challenging the propriety of God's prohibitions. And it involves setting oneself apart from God and living independently from God, with one's own self as the center. This is the ultimate misuse of human freedom. This distrusting self-centeredness takes two primary forms. The first, pride, is something that we are very familiar with. Pride is the willful refusal to live in creaturely dependence upon God. We want to usurp God's role as Lord, and we want to rule over our own lives and the lives of others. Unlike prideful overreaching, the second form of this self-centered lack of faith takes the form of despairing self-loathing and self-hatred. In the case of pride we refuse to live in needy dependence on God, and we need to be brought low by God. In the case of self-loathing we refuse believe that we are cared for and loved by a gracious and merciful God, and we must be raised up by God. In both cases it is a lack of faith and trust in God that leads to self-centeredness and self-preoccupation. The end result is that we live lives that are against what God intends for his creatures. Our fellowship and communion with God is broken.

> **Total Depravity.** Total depravity does not mean that we are as bad as we possibly can be, nor does it mean that we commit every sin. It means that sin refers not merely to the individual acts of a person, but that it refers primarily to the person's life as a whole—sin is comprehensive and total. We read in the New Testament that we are "dead in [our] trespasses" (Ephesians 2:1, 5 NIV), "by nature children of wrath" (Ephesians 2:3) and "slaves to sin" (Romans 6:16, 19-20 NIV). Since no portion or aspect of us is free from the corruption of sin, we are completely incapable of saving ourselves—we must rely totally upon God's grace to regenerate us—to give us new birth.

Is "sinning" who I am or what I do?

The traditional or classical articulation of the doctrine of sin identifies two closely related definitions of sin—"actual sin" and "original sin."

"Actual sin" refers to a set of acts done against God's law or will. "Original sin" names our condition. We are responsible for the various sins we perform. This responsibility is not and cannot be removed or minimized by reference to our sinful condition. Whatever original sin implies, sin cannot be considered a fate before which we are finally helpless and without responsibility.

However, if we only talk about the specific sins we perform, then we risk viewing sin in purely individualistic and moralistic terms. Viewing sin this way leads to viewing salvation as simply replacing our sinful actions with good actions. Each of us could, theoretically, stop sinning by trying harder. In this case, what we need as a remedy for our predicament is more willpower, not a crucified savior.

Here we see the interrelatedness of the doctrine of salvation and the doctrine of sin. In a real sense, we must begin with the doctrine of salvation and the remedy for our predicament, in order to see the gravity of our sin. If we begin with Jesus' death by crucifixion, then we see the serious nature of our sin and our sinful condition. We also see the power of God's grace and mercy as God confronts and defeats sin.

As we consider how best to hold together the sins that we perform and our condition as sinners, we must also address the question of the relationship between the sin of Adam and the sin of every other human being. The issue at hand is whether in affirming the reality of our sinful condition we also must think that we inherited sin and guilt from Adam. If we have a strong notion of the connection between Adam's sin and our own, and we use the language of inheritance or hereditary sin, then we risk using the category of original sin as an alibi. "Do not blame me," we might say. "It is all Adam's fault; there is nothing that I can do." We need to speak of sin in such a way that we do not limit our responsibility and accountability for the sin we perform. We cannot talk of original sin in such a way that it provides us with an alibi. This encourages our tendency of always finding a way to blame someone else.

Let's look at Romans 5:12, "Therefore, just as sin came into the world through one man, and death came through sin, and so death spread to all because all have sinned." It is clear from this passage that both sin and death are universal. However, what remains unclear is the relation of Adam's sin to the sins and death of everyone else. We read that sin came into the world through *one* man; and, we read that death spread to all because *all* have sinned. Paul stresses the universal impact of Adam's sin and he emphasizes the fault of every human person. We must not put all the weight on Adam's sin and then neglect to recognize our own responsibility for our own sin. Yet we cannot dismiss any connection between Adam's sin and everyone else's sin. So, we ought to affirm that there indeed was an original act of sin, and sin entered the world through this first act of sin, and with sin—spiritual death. We must reject a view (Pelagianism) that says that Adam was simply a bad influence and example, which we may or may not follow. No, sin is universal—it is a condition in which we find ourselves due to Adam's sin, but sin is also something that we do and for which we are responsible. At this point we see the limitations of language of inherited guilt, hereditary sin and sin as a contagion that is somehow physically transmitted from generation to generation. Sin is not a genetic disposition. Sin refers to distorted and broken personal relations with God and my neighbor. Sin is an unquestionable universal reality, yet I am accountable for my own sin. We destroy our own lives through our own acts.

Vocation. Typically we think of vocation in terms of career, profession and job. Instead, we ought to think of it as living in faithful obedience to God's call on our lives. Vocation refers to living in ways that glorify God, serve others and participate in God's mission in the world. We are called and commissioned to be servants of God and followers of Jesus in the world. This is a type of existence in which we live not in our own name and for our own sake. Rather, we live as servants of the world in the name of God. Our vocation is to lose our lives for Jesus' sake, and in doing so we will find our true lives (Matthew 10:39). And it is in living a life worthy of our calling (Ephesians 4:1) that we come to the fullness of our identities in Christ, as empowered by the Holy Spirit.

Is sin the most essential truth about us?

With all of this talk about sin, does this mean that Christians are pessimists? Are we really all miserable wretches? Should we constantly engage in self-examination so that we can identify all the sin in our lives and confess our faults before God?

We certainly need to take sin seriously. In fact, we need to reintroduce the words "sin" and "guilt" in our Christian vocabulary. There has been great theological slippage in recent years, as the church has moved away from offensive and harsh words in favor of using less threatening words to describe our situation. We are no longer guilty; now our lives are simply meaningless. We do not perform acts of sin in need of forgiveness; now we make mistakes or do things that show poor judgment. That said, we should not become preoccupied with our sin. We should not wallow in our sinfulness, brokenness and wretchedness. Instead, we should live confidently in the gospel of Jesus and the forgiveness of sins.

We must speak of ourselves as sinners and yet affirm that sin is not finally definitive of who we are. We must recognize that even though sin is a significant element of the Bible it is not its main theme. We should not consider the reality of sin and ourselves as sinners apart from the saving work of God in Christ, which leads to the forgiveness of sin, our liberation from the clutches of sin, and our being recreated as new creatures.

In a letter to his friend and colleague Philipp Melanchthon, the great sixteenth-century reformer Martin Luther wrote these compelling, yet often misunderstood, words, "Be a sinner and sin boldly, but believe and rejoice in Christ even more boldly, for he is victorious over sin, death, and the world."[4] These words are misunderstood if we think that Luther is suggesting that we should have no concern regarding our sin, that we should be brazen in our sinfulness. No. Luther is too good of a student of Paul. He is certainly not suggesting that we persist in our sinning so that grace may abound more and more, a suggestion to which Paul responds with an emphatic "No!" (Romans 6:1-2). Here Luther is telling us to be honest with ourselves. Admit that we sin and that we are sinners. It is better to boldly sin, according to Luther, than it is to desperately try to cover up our sins, or strive futilely to cease from sinning on the strength of our own power alone. We should sin boldly by admitting to others, ourselves and God that we are indeed sinners. But, we then need to move immediately to living confidently in the victorious work of Christ. We are sinners, yes. But, we are sinners saved by grace. When we acknowledge that we are sinners, we can stop pretending to be people we are not. When we embrace the fact that we have been saved by grace, we can stop wallowing in our sinfulness, and give up on our lives of self-deprecating accusation. We are able then to live in the freedom of God's victory over sin, as the people God intends and enables us to be.

The Heidelberg Catechism

Q. 1 What is your only comfort, in life and in death?

A. That I belong—body and soul, in life and in death—not to myself but to my faithful Savior, Jesus Christ, who at the cost of his own blood has fully paid for all my sins and has completely freed me from the dominion of the devil; that he protects me so well that without the will of my Father in heaven not a hair can fall from my head; indeed, that everything must fit his purpose for my salvation. Therefore, by his Holy Spirit, he also assures me of eternal life, and makes me wholeheartedly willing and ready from now on to live for him.

Q. 2 How many things must you know that you may live and die in the blessedness of this comfort?

A. Three. First, the greatness of my sin and wretchedness. Second, how I am freed from all my sins and their wretched consequences. Third, what gratitude I owe to God for such redemption.[5]

10

WHO IS THE CHURCH?

Daniel J. Treier

Our title reminds us to ask *who*, not just *what*, because the church is neither a building nor just an institution—it is the whole people of God. The church is the newly recreated people of Israel that now includes all who participate in the life of Jesus Christ. In the third "article" of the Nicene Creed, the final section devoted to the Holy Spirit, we note that the church is one, holy, catholic and apostolic. Oneness points to the church's unity; holiness, to being set apart for serving God; catholicity, to each part being connected to all the gifts of whole; apostolicity, to being faithfully connected with the apostles' teaching and mission. Of course, these marks are true of the church only in a preliminary sense, anticipating fullness of life in the world to come.

The key term, *ekklesia*, refers to an assembly. The church is the community of people who respond when the Holy Spirit calls them to gather as followers of Jesus Christ. We are called out of "the world," yes; but more centrally we are called together, into communion with each other as we are united to God in Christ. The church ought to show the world what it means to be the world—that is, what the fellowship humans are created for should actually look like.

The New Testament teaches about the church through a dazzling array of images. The church is a temple, a household, a bride, a vineyard and much more. At root the church is the people of God who participate in the life of Christ, and therefore share in each others' lives, by the Spirit. Thus the church fulfills what the Old Testament anticipates: "My dwelling place will be with them; I will be their God, and they will be my people"

(Ezekiel 37:27 NIV). We share humanly in the fellowship that characterizes the triune God as Father, Son and Holy Spirit.

Hence church is not just what we do, but who we are. Church is a "missional" reality: as the Father sent the Son into the world, so now by the Spirit the Son sends us into the world. We are sent not just to *worship* God, *nurture* each other and bear *witness* to society in word and deed—although these are the basic relational activities of the church. We are also sent simply to be God's people, embodying the good news by our very presence in the world as forgiven and forgiving sinners. The mission is God's; we are privileged to be a sign, pointing toward the coming of God's kingdom in its fullness.

Different models of the church are especially prominent in various Christian traditions. Catholic and Orthodox Christians, along with some Protestants, emphasize the church being (1) an institution, highlighting the "apostolic succession" of bishops who connect Christians historically back to the apostles. Such Christians also tend to see the church as (2) a mystical communion, highlighting the "communion of saints" across time and place. Another influential model in those traditions is the church as (3) sacrament, highlighting the ways the church brings God's gracious presence to the world.

Many Protestants emphasize less vertical, more horizontal models. Martin Luther and others associated strongly with the Reformation era provide a bridge to these models with emphasis on the church as (4) herald—proclaiming God's word. Still vertically inclined, this model nevertheless moves away from centralizing church authority in its institutional or mystical being, focusing instead on a crucial act of the church. Other, "lower-church," Protestants such as Anabaptists—and some Catholic "liberation theologies"—emphasize the church as (5) servant, highlighting the work of local congregations seeking justice and peace. Still other Protestants see the church primarily as (6) a community of disciples, highlighting the pursuit of personal and social holiness.

The church is all that these models, with their differing emphases, suggest. Word and sacrament, central as they are to both worship and witness, therefore become especially crucial marks identifying the church; word and sacrament are activities that shape its distinctive being.

But noting the church's "one, holy, catholic and apostolic" character points to another mark alongside word and sacrament: order. Order marks out the church in terms of its membership, leadership and practices of life together—plus, for the time being, the geographical and theological variety by which "the church" exists as particular churches. Thanks to church order we may offer God true worship, each other true love and the world true service—faithful to the good news of Christ's redeeming presence with estranged sinners in word and sacrament.

(Why) do Christians (have to) go to church?!

This question often surfaces after students have been away from home for a while, trying various churches and connecting deeply with none. Meanwhile, they tell me, their most profound experience of Christian community emerged in college dorm life. Indeed, the church is not the fullness of God's kingdom; the Holy Spirit upholds creation and culture too.

But the church is the preeminent sign of God's work in the world. If

Cyprian—"Outside the church there is no salvation."[1] This famous saying, *extra Ecclesiam nulla salus* ("Outside the church there is no salvation"), is cited approvingly not just in Catholic and Orthodox churches but also (despite different interpretations) by Protestant Reformers. Indeed, John Calvin affirmed that to have God as our father we must have the church as our mother.[2]

Saint Cyprian was a highly educated convert to Christianity who became Bishop at Carthage for a decade until his martyrdom. This saying comes from Epistle 72 to Jubaianus, "Concerning the Baptism of Heretics." Upholding the catholicity of the one true church, Cyprian denied the legitimacy of baptisms among heretics. While God deals graciously with ignorance, connection to the true church remains vital. For salvation brings people into communion with the true God rejected by the heretics and revealed in Christ. Therefore, as Christ's body, the church is essential for experiencing what salvation truly is.

Jesus says that our love for each other is what makes us distinct, then "Lone Ranger Christians" cannot bear such witness alone. While individuals might worship in their "prayer closets," they cannot fulfill the divine goal of a people that will declare God's glory among the nations (Psalm 96:3). Parachurch organizations help extend the church's ministry in certain areas (like education) and bring different Christians together wonderfully. But they don't provide the kind of long-term accountability that God locates in local congregations. I participate in my church—warts and all—to get ready for the fullness of God's kingdom.

How can the church point to Jesus' love when we're such a sinful mess?

Yes, there are clergy abuse scandals, declining and divided denominations and worship wars. At college we used to get up from the lunch table with the line, "Let's make like a Baptist church and split." (You should feel free to replace "Baptist" with your own kind of church.) Theologians talk about the church too much with ideal concepts, so we need more confession of personal and corporate sin along with less triumphalism. In different ways the Catholic and Orthodox traditions remind us, though, that the gates of hell shall not prevail: God has promised to build the church and will not let her comprehensively fail. From a Protestant perspective, this doesn't provide guarantees for any particular institutional arrangement, but it also doesn't authorize us to abandon a church at the first sign of trouble. The church, like its members, is *simul iustus et peccator*: simultaneously justified and still sinful. If the church weren't sinful it would be empty: don't join the perfect one or you'll ruin it.

Evangelical Protestants, at our worst, quickly flee sinful institutions and start new ones. We hope they will be as pure as the primitive church of the apostles, yet we are soon disappointed, time after time. However, at our best, we can be agents of renewal within otherwise complacent forms of church life. House church and new monastic movements today highlight aspects of what the church should strive to be, reflecting the small, close-knit congregations in the New Testament. Like any charismatic communities, though, to survive over time and to connect across space they must institutionalize somewhat—just like the early church did as it started to move toward more "catholic" forms.

After all, the New Testament itself portrays churches that are far from perfect. No matter how charismatic or institutional, a Christian congregation points to the love of Christ by being forgiven, not perfect.

Me + friends + Starbucks or guitar = church?

Jesus promises in Matthew 18:20 to be among us when two or three gather in his name. Yet the Holy Spirit indwells each person and God is everywhere. This always made me wonder what's special about being together that can't happen when Christians are apart.

The Matthew passage has a particular context: church discipline, when someone doesn't respond to efforts seeking reconciliation, and the church has to decide how to proceed. As the congregation addresses testimony from two or three witnesses, Jesus is present—even in difficult deliberations. The important point is that Jesus builds his church, being present in whatever ways we need. Corporate worship throughout the Bible, the sacraments, even the praise already taking place in heaven—all these factors suggest that God meets us in a special way when we gather. In fact, some "temple" passages about the Holy Spirit's indwelling may have congregations in view, not just individuals.

What is worship, and why go to "war" over the presence or absence of liturgy?

Worship is the covenant people meeting with their God. Worship has movement. God calls people together. As we respond in praise, acknowledging God's awesome character, we recognize our sinfulness. God receives our confession and restores fellowship, announcing once again that we are forgiven. Then we can greet one another, sharing God's peace as agents of reconciliation. We continue our praise, bringing gifts for God's work, and offering prayers for one another and the world. In all this we prepare to hear God's Word read and then proclaimed.

Having heard from God afresh, we respond. We receive a blessing, being sent out again to serve God in the world. Celebrating the Lord's Supper, we receive God's grace as we remember Christ's work, reaffirm our unity, and renew our hope for a heavenly banquet enjoying the fullness of God's kingdom.

Every church has liturgy: liturgy simply involves patterns for worship's movement. Some liturgies are formal and planned, while others are freer yet still learned through practice. All worship needs both form and freedom. Forms like written prayers help us to learn the wisdom of past saints and present teachers, to have the gospel implanted more deeply into hearts and minds. Freedom helps us to recognize the Holy Spirit in our midst, to realize that God leads the church as a living tradition into the future. My own experience seems to be more and more common among younger generations: formal elements of liturgy actually give me the freedom to find God with others.

Worship is not solely praise offered in song, or feelings experienced in praise. Worship is a set of practices for offering ourselves to God while also receiving grace anew—hearing, seeing and tasting, as well as speaking and singing. These practices express feelings but also reshape them. Worship seems boring when we forget that God is present—or when, instead of the good news, we focus on our individual experiences. The right mix of form and freedom can help the gospel drama to come alive for us.

What is so special about the "the sacraments"?

Sacraments are mysteries, rituals that function as embodied signs helping us to participate in God's grace. Baptists and other "low-church" groups usually speak of "ordinances" instead, emphasizing human obedience rather than divine mystery. Most Protestants believe that just two items fit this category, whatever we call it—baptism and the Lord's Supper (or "Eucharist," which means thanksgiving). However, some Anglicans speak of more than two sacraments, even to the point of affirming all seven sacraments of the Catholic church: Baptism, Confirmation, Holy Eucharist, Penance, Anointing of the Sick, Holy Orders, Matrimony.

Even those who speak of ordinances can grant that God graciously meets his people when they celebrate them. Protestants like myself, who speak of only two sacraments, can grant that marriage is a means of God's transforming grace (oh boy, is it ever!), and so are lots of other

Baptism, Eucharist, and Ministry. "Baptism, Eucharist, and Ministry" comes from the Faith and Order Commission of the World Council of Churches.[3] Recognizing that these subjects are at the heart of division among churches, the document expresses a degree of convergence, seeking to move ecumenical efforts forward. Baptism is the basis of the whole people of God being called into ministry. Ordained ministry is a distinct calling but no more important than that of the lay people it represents and serves. Accordingly,

> In the celebration of the eucharist, Christ gathers, teaches and nourishes the Church. It is Christ who invites to the meal and who presides at it. . . . The one who presides at the eucharistic celebration in the name of Christ makes clear that the rite is not the assemblies' own creation or possession; the eucharist is received as a gift from Christ living in his Church.[4]

The result is a doctrine of the church that makes *koinonia*—"fellowship," with God in Christ and among us—central.

experiences. Yet the Bible connects baptism and the Lord's Supper distinctively in 1 Corinthians 10–11, where they share distinctive association with Christ's work on the cross. Marriage and other "sacraments" mysteriously connect us to Christ, but they don't symbolize or remind us of his work on the cross in the same way.

The sacraments highlight that God saves whole people—not just minds, but bodies. And God saves people in community—not just receiving grace privately, but also sharing in salvation publicly with others. Plus God saves us forever—not just forgiving past personal sins, but also reconciling us to each other and ultimately making all things new.

But isn't eleven o'clock Sunday morning the most segregated hour in America?

This is a very important but difficult question. Michael Emerson and

Christian Smith explain that evangelicals wrongly assume one-on-one relationships will heal our racially divided society.[5] But there is also structural evil and systemic sin. When my conservative African American friend had to reject an invitation because he feared he would undergo racial profiling, I started to realize how naive I was about a supposedly colorblind focus on personal responsibility. Emerson and Smith call for developing intentionally multi-ethnic congregations to raise the kind of awareness I lacked, and also to reconcile divided groups through acts of solidarity.

Galatians 3:28 points to the hope of every tribe and tongue praising God with their distinctive gifts. True unity rejoices in God-honoring diversity. Unity is no excuse for assimilating minority groups into still majority-dominant cultures. But we also can't settle for supposedly "separate but equal" tribalism. For some white Christians to give up the comfort of familiarity and join minority congregations may be a first step toward reconciliation.

Who's (really) the boss?

It's easy to notice that Jesus doesn't seem to be the head of his body—or at least our human bureaucracies get longer and longer necks! Jesus gave authority—the keys of the kingdom—to his apostles. Yet even their lifetimes were filled with churchly chaos and power grabs, as the New Testament repeatedly demonstrates. Just read 1 Corinthians!

Again we need both form and freedom. Congregationally-governed churches recognize only two biblical "offices": pastors and deacons. Pastors lead by teaching, and deacons lead in serving, while congregations make decisions as a whole. Emphasis is on strictest possible adherence to explicit biblical forms of governance.

Presbyterian churches distinguish two types of elders in 1 Timothy 5:17: teaching and ruling. Teaching elders function similarly to pastors in other traditions; ruling elders form a congregational session, and elders in a region of churches or presbytery form a synod that acts together beyond the congregation.

Episcopal churches find freedom to move one step farther in the direction they think the later New Testament churches (or "early catholicism") headed. Particular leaders of leaders in regional or city churches (collections of house congregations)—bishops—after the apostles' deaths provided the closest analogue to apostolic authority binding various churches together across time and place. Bishops don't minister salvation in Christ's place but simply extend the apostles' shepherding ministry into our own day.

No form of church polity can claim exact equivalence with early Christian practice or easy extraction from biblical proof-texts. The question is what mix of parallel forms and cultural freedom does the most justice to the New Testament functions of church leadership. Even more important is the character of these church leaders: will they be gentle shepherds like Jesus? I have been blessed to have several pastors like that; I've also seen moments of bullying rather than feeding the sheep. Similarly, I know of bureaucratic structures—deacon boards, sessions of elders, and even groups of bishops—that ministered the godly wisdom of multiple counselors, while others followed paths to cultural power rather than the way of the cross. Healthy structures can be helpful, but they are no substitute for the Holy Spirit's work in the lives of our leaders.

When, if ever, should Christians separate?

I do not exaggerate when I say that the most painful moments of my life have involved divisions between Christians. I hope this does not become your experience too; but it might. It may help to see that the New Testament portrays different kinds of divisions.

1. Regarding the gospel, with separation sometimes necessary due to resisting false teachers. Gospel-level divisions typically involve heretical Christology—denial of Christ's divine lordship or his full humanity in Jesus.

2. Regarding ministry, with separation sometimes necessary due to differing approaches. Paul and Barnabas disagreed about whether to take Mark along after his earlier desertion. Eventually, rather than remaining paralyzed in disagreement, they took different partners. Sometimes God multiplies ministry in this fallen world after charitable separations in which fellowship remains intact. Maybe this category offers a paradigm for at least some denominational differences today. I happily teach with

friends from various denominations and numerous local churches; we share fellowship and common Christian work at the college even if we practice our evangelical faith differently.

3. Regarding *adiaphora* or "disputable matters," with separation unnecessary. Passages like Romans 14–15 suggest that in many cases, while challenging one another graciously, we should grant each other freedom to live out various understandings of God's Word, finding ways for our congregations to remain both like-minded and personally accountable to God. My local congregation is a wonderful source of challenge and blessing even though I disagree with some of its official theology and ministry initiatives.

Today's denominational divisions can be particularly challenging when official statements retain orthodox Christology while certain churches and leaders may not. Moreover, Jude, among other Scriptures, relates promotion of sexual immorality with denying the lordship of Christ, while 1 John implies that failure to love is also connected to Christological error. Aspects of both "progressive" and "conservative" ethical commitments have implications for how we relate to Jesus. How then does the first category above—gospel-level divisions—apply in these contemporary contexts? We likely need categories two and three to address that question, since the Bible doesn't directly anticipate our forms of church division. Some Christians will discern a call to separate, others to stay. Each group may have legitimate reasons for their decisions.

Infant baptism: does God have grandchildren?

Baptism initiates believers into our "priestly" role and publicly signals our membership in Christ's body as we share in the Holy Spirit. Thanks to baptism (and, often for baptized infants, later confirmation) we may share in the Lord's Supper, being subject to the church's nurture and discipline.

Opponents of paedobaptism (that is, baptizing infants) emphasize confession of faith in New Testament baptism passages. I've heard them use the slogan I referenced in the question above, saying that Christian children can't ride into heaven on their parents' coattails. More recent defenses of paedobaptism acknowledge this need for faith to be present.

The question remains whether this faith must belong directly to the baptized person, or instead to the church and the family on the child's behalf. Paedobaptists suggest that "household" texts like Acts 16, and the Old Testament parallel of circumcision, support this idea of God's blessing on children who are connected to the covenant community.

Orthodox, Catholic, Lutheran and some Anglican paedobaptists find baptism to be "regenerating," the occasion for receiving new life in Christ and having the guilt of original sin removed. Reformed and Methodist paedobaptists typically reject baptismal regeneration, seeing baptism instead as "sign and seal" of God's promises, anticipating the child's growth toward personally embracing faith.

Nominal faith is a problem for every Christian community. Paedobaptism is no guarantee that a child will depersonalize spiritual life, just as a conversion experience offers no guarantee that a person will persevere in faith.

Does increasing cultural engagement and attention to social justice mean losing the heart of the gospel?

There is real wisdom in the saying that we must be in the world but not of it. We should not treat evangelism and social action as inevitably competing priorities. Yes, we must maintain commitment to gospel witness. But we must also realize that social action isn't just a pragmatic means to evangelistic ends; it is part of living out the gospel itself.

The church must be close enough to minister in the world—doing good to all, especially the household of faith (Galatians 6:10). The church must remain far enough from the world to minister *Christ* and not just "culture"—the city on a hill must let light shine; the salt must be savory enough to preserve and heal (Matthew 5:13-16). We return to the perennial dynamic of form and freedom.

A former pastor of mine said we can imagine the world to be the water and the church a boat. The world is God's gift, the necessary environment for life. Yet this water always pushes against the boat, filling whatever space it can. The church seems to be full of holes, always at risk of sinking into the world. But God keeps the church afloat as a lifeboat, rescuing people so they can then fish for others (Matthew 4:19).

It is significant that family is a central image for the church in Scripture. The church is our "first family," the primary context in which we grow into true humanity together (Ephesians 4:13-16). The gospel and the church are not at odds: God forgives us in Christ so that by the Holy Spirit we can minister forgiveness to each other (Matthew 6:12). The church is supposed to welcome people into the family of God and *to be* that family, looking forward to a great reunion!

The Lausanne Covenant. Lausanne promotes, in the words of an internet tagline, "The Whole Church taking the Whole Gospel to the Whole World."[6] The 1974 International Congress on World Evangelization at Lausanne in Switzerland was spearheaded by Billy Graham and John R. W. Stott but attended by leaders from over 150 countries. Its public covenant begins with God's purpose to call a holy people from every nation, affirming the Bible's authority, Christ's uniqueness and universality, and the nature of evangelism as proclamation.

Articles then follow addressing Christian social responsibility in a holistic relationship with evangelism:

Here too we express penitence both for our neglect and for having sometimes regarded evangelism and social concern as mutually exclusive. Although reconciliation with other people is not reconciliation with God, nor is social action evangelism, nor is political liberation salvation, nevertheless we affirm that evangelism and sociopolitical involvement are both part of our Christian duty.[7]

11

HOW SHOULD I LIVE?

Vincent Bacote

During my time in college and years immediately following graduation, I found myself in a struggle to understand what it meant to live as a faithful Christian. I was familiar with concepts like discipleship and words like *witness* but it was not always clear to me what this meant for my life from day to day. Of course I knew that it was important to be a person who attempted to share the faith with others and to be someone who cultivated a deepening personal relationship with God, but beyond this I was not always certain about what it meant to live as a Christian beyond evangelism and the pursuit of personal piety.

At times this felt like an acute crisis, because I wanted to live a life that pleased God more than anything else (at least most of the time). At that time of my life I was often susceptible to being persuaded, at least temporarily, by the most recent encounter with a passionate Christian who seemed to know exactly what all Christians should do with their lives. After a while, the crisis would often manifest itself like a battle of competing voices in my head, all of which seemed to have very good reasons for pointing me toward God's will for my life. The voices represented the views of family, peers, parachurch leaders and famous pastors; I wasn't sure how to move forward at times because I wondered if God would be disappointed if I chose one path over another. This sometimes happened in situations like choosing whether or not I should attend a rock concert by a non-Christian band.

I can remember vividly one occasion when the crisis was particularly acute. I heard some voices say "have a good time" while others would say "aren't you supporting people who espouse a lifestyle that's not like yours?" I chose to attend the concert after much vexation and had a nice time, but I did have some ambivalence after deciding that it was all right to buy a ticket and attend the show.

While a decision about concert attendance may seem trivial, the thought process that I experienced lays bare the fact that the Christian life is a life that should be taken very seriously. If we are people who belong to God, shouldn't we care what God thinks about the decisions we make in life? Shouldn't we care about how we live?

Another way to think about this is to say that what we believe as Christians needs to be linked to how we go about our lives each day, and that this is a task that sometimes presents us with vexing questions, sometimes to the point of personal crisis, as in my circumstance. It can be a more difficult process of discernment than we might anticipate. Each day we are faced with many decisions related to our priorities in life and the manner and status of our interpersonal relationships. While we may have familiarity (or increasingly so) with the Bible and with theological words like creation, eschatology and sanctification, how does it play out in the way that we should conduct ourselves? How does it lead us to decide which turn to take at the forks in the path of life? Discernment is necessary if we desire to live lives characterized by faithfulness to God. Christians often find themselves in debates and long conversations about life discernment, perhaps especially when it comes to things like politics, participation in the culture around us and personal decisions like marriage, career and lifestyle. How shall we now live? How can we have faith as a way of life, both public and private? The questions that follow are hardly exhaustive, but they represent some of the conversations we have with students regularly around hard questions.

Why should I care about the world?

"Be holy, because I am holy" (1 Peter 1:16).

"Do not love the world" (1 John 2:15).

"Friendship with the world is hatred toward God" (James 4:4).

Biblical phrases like these leave little to the imagination, especially when we read them in context. God wants his people to be set apart to him, to stand out from those who are not in a covenant relationship with him. When God commands us to be holy, he is telling us that we should be people whose lives are distinctive, but it is not always easy to know what that "looks" like. I sometimes wonder what would happen if I asked students or a congregation to close their eyes and imagine what a holy person looks like. Given that holiness has to do with purity and being set apart to God, I wonder if the person who appears in their mind's eye is some man or woman who either lived in another time and place or whether it is a contemporary person whose appearance says "Amish."

Holiness is so often associated with separation that it can lead us to think of it primarily in terms of how our belonging to God takes us away from anything we would regard as other than "spiritual." One way this can manifest itself is that fidelity to the gospel can be interpreted to mean that college is only preparation for ministry (and there are Bible verses that can be read in a way that supports this view) and serious attention to science or the humanities is indicative of misplaced priorities. This can also be seen when Christian engagement in culture or deep investment in one's career path is seen as worldliness.

What is a Christian to do? God clearly calls us to be holy, but the distinctiveness that emerges in practical holiness does not mean a denial of the creation that God pronounced "very good" in Genesis 1:31. To be worldly is to live in God's creation with disregard for the one who designed this universe. Holiness is participation in God's creation, whether this is athletics, art, education, medicine or law. If we take the doctrine of creation seriously along with our doctrine of salvation, we are on a path that leads us to see holiness as the process toward living more and more like a true human being. After all, humans are God's idea; holiness that sets us apart is humanness that increasingly reflects what God intended for humans as they fully participate in the world he created.

Should I care about politics?

A survey released prior to the 2012 US general presidential election indicated that Millennials (those ages 18 to 25 at the time of the election) were less than optimistic about political participation: "Overall, younger Millennials exhibit a high degree of pessimism about the democratic process and government. More than six in ten (63 percent) of the Millennials agree that 'people like me don't have any say about what the government does,' while more than eight in ten (82 percent) believe that business corporations have too much influence on the political process."[1] This cynicism about politics comes after a period where evangelicals had mostly overcome an ambivalence to political participation extending back to the first third of the twentieth century. By the late 1990s evangelicals tended to be positive about Christian political participation; but the first decade of the new millennium raised questions for many Christians. Is it worth participating in politics? Isn't politics really about grabbing power and using it to win a culture war, and should we even be fighting a culture war?

Politics is one domain of public engagement where some Christians see abundant reason for thinking "maybe I should just opt out of this one," but such decisions should not be made hastily by Christians who live in countries where citizens have voting rights, where corruption is not the law of the land and where public service in political office is a possibility. James W. Skillen, founder of the Center for Public Justice, offers a helpful perspective when he reminds us that politics exists not simply for the sake of politics but actually for the purpose of government:

> God has repeatedly called his people to recognize that government is "God's servant for your good" and that it does not bear the sword in vain. (Romans 13:4). God has also repeatedly sent prophets to call governments to account for not fulfilling their God-given duty to uphold justice (Read Isaiah 10:1-4 or Jeremiah 22:1-23 for example).[2]

Government is accountable to God, and politics at its best should be seen as the way we work together toward establishing a government that lives up to its purpose of serving the public good and establishing justice.

When we think about politics, it is important for us to consider what God has revealed about governments and the obligations of his people. At the least, we should care about politics because the Bible reveals to us that God cares about justice and because we are commanded to pray for our political leaders (and in the first century these were not usually friends of the church). To care about politics is ultimately to care about the life we share with other human beings; political life is an imperfect expression of multilevel efforts to order our common life in a way that reflects justice and leads to human flourishing. It often falls far short of this lofty aim, but political failures are more reason for us to pray for wisdom for our leaders and for ourselves as we have opportunities and responsibilities to vote, participate in local and national campaigns, make our opinions heard at town halls and maybe even run for office, all as an expression of fidelity to our God who calls for justice.

Of course, if you have enough conversations about Christians and political action, it will become clear that there are a range of postures Christians take toward this form of engagement in the world. The approach above is reflective of a view some call "transformational" and is associated with the legacy of John Calvin and Abraham Kuyper (who rose to Prime Minister of the Netherlands in 1901). There are other Christians who regard participation in the political realm as part of life in this world, but without any clear aim to bring about Christian "influence" or change to social and political structures. These Christians follow what some call the "Two Kingdoms" approach of Martin Luther; the Kingdom of God is tied to the gospel and our life in the church, and the Kingdom of the World is tied to the law God gave to his people that only functions to reveal the fact of sin and to restrain its influence in the lives of individuals and society (but the law does not save anyone). Still other Christians place a high emphasis on their allegiance to Jesus to the extent that engagement in political structures is seen as either too risky or as a compromise to faithful discipleship. Some who call themselves Mennonites or Anabaptist embody this emphasis. Yet a different angle can be seen in the practice of those who regard their public speech and action as a prophetic gesture that may be limited to protest but may go as far as being a catalyst for change. Some African American Christians across denominations have identified with this approach.

While not exhaustive, the previous paragraph reveals that Christians have given much thought and action to political engagement. Multiple factors may influence where Christians land on this question. While it may seem to be one of the most difficult to face, we should consider it an opportunity to think together with fellow Christians about how we honor God and pursue the good in human society. Don't despair; exhale and take your time thinking through this one.

Abraham Kuyper (1837–1920). Abraham Kuyper began his career as a pastor and eventually became Prime Minister of the Netherlands. He was involved in the life of the church as well as politics and education. He edited a weekly and daily paper for over forty years, wrote devotionals, helped found a Christian university (The Free University of Amsterdam) and sought to encourage Christians to participate in public life while also emphasizing their distinctiveness. He was a unique figure who sought to honor God by seeking to bring Christian influence into politics and culture. He is an intriguing example of someone whose passion for God led him to live out his faith in a very public way.

Does being Christian mean membership in a specific political party?

I am an African American, born in 1965, the year after the major Civil Rights Act was put into law by President Lyndon Johnson, a Democrat. By the time I was aware of what voting meant, it was clear among my immediate family and relatives that there was only one way to vote. My family raised me in a Baptist background, and faith was very important to me. When I went to college and became part of an evangelical Bible study, it was a great surprise to me to find that everyone seemed in favor of the Republican Party. My response at that time was to commit to a conspiracy of silence and not discuss my confusion about which party a Christian should support.

Many friends and students have told me stories of similar moments of dissonance when they encountered fellow believers equally committed to the faith but on the opposite side of political affiliation. For some, these encounters are often intense, especially when people believe it is "obvious" that a Christian would affiliate with a particular party. What makes it obvious? Whether one identifies as Republican, Democrat or Libertarian, the respective Christian adherents find the party of their choice to adhere to principles or pursue policies that accord with their understanding of the way biblical commitments would find political expression. One way to think about this is by considering what people think of when they have a commitment to "justice." The reason my relatives have tended to support Democrats is because they have been the party that has given significant attention to racial justice in the last half-century, while many evangelicals have supported Republicans in recent decades because of attention to issues such as abortion and religious freedom. In both cases there is a belief that the political party of choice best attends to the government's charge to do justice, though the specific expressions of justice are in different domains that people find important and that they believe are public concerns that should matter to Christians. Yet strong disagreement remains among Christians when it comes to party affiliation.

What's a Christian to do? First, we should keep in mind that our expectations of politics should be tempered by the recognition that no human activities should be confused with bringing about the kind of perfect society that will only arrive when Christ returns and establishes the eternal kingdom. While we wait for Christ to come and make all things right, we should earnestly seek justice and strive to wisely evaluate the political commitments and strategies of those serving the public (or hoping to do so) from each party. Chances are Christians will have good reasons for aligning with one party or another; a Christian consensus on politics is most likely unattainable before Christ returns. This means those awkward conversations will go on, but it is important to use these moments of dissonance as opportunities for listening to our brothers and sisters. If you cannot imagine why a Christian would ever vote Democrat, Republican or even the Green Party, inquire with sincerity and curiosity instead of suspicion. This is not always easy, especially when a passion for justice is involved, but here we find an opportunity for Christians to lead the way as models of civility. Affiliating with a political party can be a positive expression of Christian faithfulness, but we have to resist confusing our political allegiance with our fidelity to the triune God.

Martin Luther King Jr.—Letter from a Birmingham Jail, April 16, 1963. Martin Luther King Jr. was faced with the question of whether a Christian should be politically active, especially someone who was an ordained minister like he was. This excerpt helps us to see why he favored action over passivity:

I have just received a letter from a white brother in Texas. He writes: "All Christians know that the colored people will receive equal rights eventually, but it is possible that you are in too great a religious hurry. It has taken Christianity almost two thousand years to accomplish what it has. The teachings of Christ take time to come to earth." Such an attitude stems from a tragic misconception of time, from the strangely rational notion that there is something in the very flow of time that will inevitably cure all ills. . . .

Human progress never rolls in on wheels of inevitability; it comes through the tireless efforts of men willing to be co-workers with God, and without this hard work, time itself becomes an ally of the forces of social stagnation. We must use time creatively, in the knowledge that the time is always ripe to do right. Now is the time to make real the promise of democracy and transform our pending national elegy into a creative psalm of brotherhood. Now is the time to lift our national policy from the quicksand of racial injustice to the solid rock of human dignity.[3]

Can a Christian serve in the military?

Full disclosure: I went to college at the Citadel, the Military College of South Carolina. Though I have not served in the military, I have many classmates who are and have been members of all branches of the armed services in the United States. That said, I am also friends with Christians who identify as pacifists or as those committed to nonviolence. It is not hard to find Christians who can make passionate and thoughtful arguments on both sides of this question. So what should a Christian think about this question that is often one of the most difficult to discern?

One way to think about answering this question is by looking at the conversion of the Roman centurion in Acts 10. Upon converting to Christianity, we see that this conversion of a Gentile was revolutionary because Peter and other Jewish believers were not anticipating Gentiles coming into the church. We do not see any language suggesting a renunciation of the centurion's responsibilities as a high ranking military officer. For some, this indicates that participation in the military is not in opposition to Christian discipleship.

A second way to think about the question is to consider statements of Jesus such as those in Matthew 5:38-47 which command us to turn the other cheek and love our enemies. Christians committed to nonviolence interpret these texts as commanding Christians to refrain from using violent means in personal relationships and also to refrain from military participation because it often requires the use of violence as a means to completing military objectives (even if these objectives are seen as "just").

The relationship between the latter verses of Romans 12:14-21 and Romans 13:1-7 brings this tension into focus as the end of Romans 12 emphasizes love of enemies and Romans 13 emphasizes submission to government authorities (with the authority established by God). Does Romans 12 lead us to regard Christian submission to the government in Romans 13 in a way that excludes the possibility of military service, and the use of the sword by the government (Romans 13:4) as only for those in government who are outside the church? Reading the text in this way would certainly eliminate Christian participation in the military. Many other Christians interpret Romans 13 as allowing or sanctioning Christian participation in the government and military in light of the text's emphasis on government's establishment by God and even the application of the word "servant" (Romans 13:4) to those who are rulers.

I favor the latter interpretation and would not discourage participation in military service, but I have considerable respect for the arguments of those with the opposite conclusion. What this means is that just as one should carefully consider issues like political participation and party affiliation, the same care and seriousness should attend consideration of military participation. Regardless of one's conclusion, conversations with those who disagree should be characterized by humility and respect for others.

How do I discover God's will for my life?

The hard questions come to us in areas that are not only "public" concerns but also in domains that are deeply personal. Most Christians would love to have a direct hotline to God so they could get specific directions on life. Alas, we have no burning bush like Moses nor angelic visitations like Mary where we can receive specific messages from God that tell us about important events in our lives. Where are we to turn if we want to know God's will, and is there a specific will of God for our lives? This is a potentially vexing question for many Christians because life decisions such as marriage (is there "the one" God has for me?) or career (am I heading to God's chosen profession for me?) have much gravity and heavily determine a large part of life. While God might privilege some of us with a divine visitation (though I haven't met anyone with this experience), one way to begin addressing this issue is by thinking about the way we view divine sovereignty and human freedom. While Christians have spilled considerable ink sorting out this issue, the important point here is that God's word tells us that he has plans for his people (see Ephesians 1:11 and 2:10, for example) while also telling us that we should be people of discernment (for example, Proverbs repeatedly urges us to seek wisdom and make life decisions accordingly). There is a plan and there is responsibility, and God does not tell us to disregard either emphasis. There is a tension that we must endure, but it is easier to manage if we remember that one of the reasons God reminds us of his sovereignty is so that we will worship him and be comforted by the fact that he is in charge of history. Human responsibility we can regard as an opportunity to grow in our knowledge of God and in our discernment.

But how do we live in this tension and pursue God's will? We can first give attention to the dimensions of God's will that are common to all of his people. In Philippians 2:12-13, Paul urges us to work out our salvation with fear and trembling, an exhortation which follows an encouragement to become like Christ, especially in the way we interact with others (as humble servants). God is explicit throughout Scripture that his people should be like him in their character. The pursuit of this aspect of God's will should always be a top priority. Yet this is not all we should think about when considering God's will; we do need to seek God when we face decisions about relationships, career, financial management and many other personal details. Prayer and the counsel of others are very important as we take steps forward with our life details. We are commanded to come to God with our requests and to seek guidance (for example, James 1:5) and we are also encouraged to participate in the community (the church visible and invisible, local and spread out). Those who know us well are used by God to help us see ourselves more truthfully and pursue our path of life with greater faithfulness (for example, Proverbs 15:22).

We also need to keep in mind that we worship a God of generosity and grace. Instead of being paralyzed by wondering if we are precisely in the center of God's will (a legitimate desire), we need to remember that God loves us more than we can imagine and that his mercy is before us. While we should seek God's will for the large and small details of our lives, we should be seeking to know the triune God who calls us his children, and who is patient with us even if the time comes when we look back over our lives and see missteps. While there is a sense in which we can say God has a specific will for us, that level of specificity often goes wanting and we need to make decisions based on our understanding of Scripture, the input of our community and personal discernment. We only have one life, so we should make our decisions carefully, but we need not be terrorized by the specter of "missing God's will" if we seem to have a path that wavers a bit. Remember that God is for us and will work things out for our good (Romans 8:28).

John Stott (1921–2011). John Stott was one of the greatest and most respected leaders in the modern evangelical movement. He was an Anglican cleric who served at All Souls Church, founded the Langham Partnership and authored more than 50 books. A superb preacher and advocate for holistic mission, his reputation as a committed, compassionate and kind person was so influential that upon death he was given tributes from those within the church and without. The reason for highlighting Stott in this chapter is not merely for these reasons, but also because he was someone who chose a life of celibacy. For Stott, the answer to the question "how should I live" included a life of singleness, a path of life to which evangelicals need to lend more respect. Regarding this he said "The gift of singleness is more a vocation than an empowerment, although to be sure God is faithful in supporting those He calls."[4]

How do I love those who are hard to love or who strongly disagree with me? Do I really have to love my enemies?

Whether it is a politician, professional athlete, church member or colleague, there are those we can generously label as "hard to love" or perhaps even as "enemies." Sometimes we encounter these people each day; at other times they are people we will never meet but we encounter them through the media. In some cases, these people directly attack us or our beliefs, and may even relish pushing our buttons, while there are other circumstances where a person seems oblivious to their behavior that may be antisocial, selfish, condescending or cruel. What do we do when put to the test by such people? Sometimes the hardest questions emerge when we are faced with people who remind us that the world remains distorted by sin.

Living with other human beings is a laboratory in sanctification (our transformation process into being Christlike), whether we love them dearly or find them insufferable. From Genesis 3 onward, humans have readily found themselves at enmity with each other, often to the point of a battle to oppress each other once sufficient power is at hand. We are tempted to find smaller and larger ways to disregard or destroy those hard to love or who are our enemies, but the way of Christ beckons us to an approach that is truly countercultural, and perhaps even counter-intuitive to many of us. Jesus instructed us to love our enemies (Matthew 5:43-48) and Paul echoes this command (Romans 12:14-21). Our com-mitment should be to live at peace with all people, and to pray for those who mistreat us (Luke 6:28). This applies not merely to people who annoy us but even to those who are truly enemies intending to harm us.

Of course, it is not a simple thing to live out this expression of sancti-fication. *Does this mean we have to be nice to everyone and never get angry?* When someone harms us, lies about us or zealously promotes an opinion we consider wrong, it makes sense for us to feel some kind of negative emotion. The challenge for us concerns our course of action when we have these experiences. The call to Christlikeness does not mean a denial of our anger or frustration. God's word directs us to tell the truth and to especially speak truthfully with fellow Christians while resisting the temptation to sin (Ephesians 4:25-27). Even if we have just reasons for anger, we do not have a "right" to settle scores. We should absolutely acknowledge the truth of the situation at hand, but this is to be followed by a response of love and compassion. We need to become well-practiced at asking how we can pray for and demonstrate love to the unlovable. Sometimes prayer alone may be all that we can do while at other times we may have opportunity to seek the good of our enemies by serving them. Sometimes we can confront the offender (or maybe send an email to that public figure), but this must be done with a view toward reconciliation and restoration.

At the time this is written, there is much handwringing about incivility in the United States and intense ideological division politically. Re-garding the latter, a student working on a political campaign told me that he heard some refer to people in the other party as "evil," which is quite a strong value judgment for an entire group of people who have a dif-ferent political strategy. Even if the label "evil" seems to be validated by the disposition and practices of those who have different views of politics or culture, those who would harm us or those who proudly blaspheme God in public, it is not our job to dehumanize them but to see them as fellow humans created in the divine image whose ultimate good we seek. When Jesus was asked to reveal the greatest commandment in the law (Matthew 22:36-40; Mark 12:28-34; Luke 10:25-28), he first said we are to love God above all else, and then followed it by the second greatest commandment: "Love your neighbor as yourself." This latter commandment must be constantly before us, especially when we are faced by those we find disagreeable, hard to love or enemies. When Jesus said this, he did not add a clause that said "except for your enemies." Who is our neighbor? Our neighbors are all human beings, near and far, friend and enemy, easy to love and seemingly impossible to love. As we get better at this hard task of sanctification, we become more like the Lord we worship and serve.

Can a Christian be wealthy?

The prosperity gospel is all around us. It is easy to find a minister on television who promises that if we have the right kind of faith we can expect blessings to follow . . . in the form of financial and material prosperity. This version of Christianity is very popular in the United States and beyond, though it might not be an exaggeration to regard it as a kind of baptized version of the American dream, where God promises to sponsor our designs for a life of abundance. There are many Christians who are critical of the prosperity gospel, yet a temptation remains in countries like the United States where the national mythology suggests that if you do enough of the right things and work hard enough, you can create your own path to success and material prosperity, and God would be pleased.

At the opposite end of the spectrum there are Christians who believe that God wants us to look at the desperation of the world around us and renounce the pursuit of material wealth in exchange for a simple approach to life with few possessions. Though it is relatively rare to find those who might commit to a lifestyle of poverty like Francis of Assisi, it is not uncommon to find Christians who believe that a faithful Christian life means resisting the desire for wealth and accumulated material goods.

Does Christian faithfulness require a renunciation of wealth? When Jesus warns us that we cannot serve two masters, he places money on the opposite side of God (Matthew 6:24), and when the rich young ruler came to him, his attachment to his wealth prevented him from following Jesus (Mark 10:17-22). We also read parables such as the rich man and Lazarus where the man with great wealth is condemned in part because he was so taken by his wealth that he ignored God's word. Yet we also see throughout the Bible that patriarchs like Abraham and Jacob were very wealthy as a result of God's blessing, and Jesus had wealthy followers like Joseph of Arimethea (though he was a secret follower during the time of Jesus' ministry).

Is the Bible of two minds on the question of wealth? Not really. Jesus warns us about the temptations associated with wealth because it can easily become a source of idolatry, but he never commands his followers to jettison money or possessions. The rich young ruler was told to give up his wealth because he had given it the place of God, but not all wealthy people were told to take such extreme measures. But we should be careful to recognize the intensity of the temptation presented by wealth. Without participating in the community of faith and keeping God our first priority, we can easily succumb and become yet another example of a Christian who claims to worship God but loves wealth even more. Wealth is not off limits for Christians, but if we fail to recognize and respect its potency trouble may likely be our companion. Wealth is a great stewardship opportunity, but we must always be aware that it is easy to find ways to rationalize our own efforts to build a kingdom in our image.

Is faithful Christian living ultimately following a book of rules from God?

When considering how we should live, one final question is how we should think about the way God wants us to follow him. Do we regard Scripture as a divine rule book, or do we primarily look for principles that set us toward a particular purpose, or should we focus our efforts on simply becoming the kind of people God wants? This can be difficult to answer: In conversations about Christian ethics, some emphasize rules, some emphasize the end result, and others emphasize the development of virtuous traits. While we can find good arguments for all three, this is one situation where we do not need to make a choice. As we pursue a life of Christian discernment and give attention to Scripture, we see that the Bible gives us commands, orients us toward a final purpose and encourages us to become virtuous people. As we grow in our understanding of the Bible and continue to improve in the way we "read" our life circumstances, we will develop greater facility in knowing how to bring these three emphases together. Because we see through a glass darkly on this side of Christ's return, we may find ourselves wrestling with the proper approach to discernment. This difficulty is not reason for despair but further motivation for us to participate in the adventurous journey of the Christian life along with our fellow brothers and sisters, seeking to know God more intimately and to practice a way of life that grows in faithfulness. As we journey down a road that may have more shifts in terrain and direction as life goes on, our discernment will continue to grow. As we get more practice, we will find ourselves getting a better sense of how we should live.

24

WHAT IS CHRISTIAN HOPE?

Beth Felker Jones

I've always been intrigued by stories that offer some horrific vision of the future. The popularity of *The Hunger Games*, Suzanne Collins's dystopia about a world gone horribly wrong, suggests that lots of us are interested in thinking about problems in the present that could easily be magnified into future disasters. Real current problems—greed, oppressive use of power, the tendency to treat bodies like objects to be bought and sold, the voyeurism of reality TV—are made larger in stories like these. In fiction, we critique the present and imagine dark futures.

But the stuff of Christian hope is a bright future, a future in which "the city does not need the sun or the moon to shine on it, for the glory of God gives it light, and the Lamb is its lamp. The nations will walk by its light, and the kings of the earth will bring their splendor into it" (Revelation 21:23-24). This is especially important in a world where it is all too easy to lose hope, to believe that the dark predictions of dystopian novels are inevitable. Hope is right at the center of Christian faith, hope for both the present and for the future.

The area of Christian teaching dealing with questions about ultimate hope is called eschatology. Eschatology is about the *eschaton*, which just means "the end." More specifically, the eschaton is God's good will for the end, God's good plan for human beings and all of creation, God's final purpose for his good work. As Christians, we trust that God is working to bring about his good intentions for all things. Historically, when Christians pay attention to eschatology, we think about four "last things": heaven, hell, death and judgment. These topics get us thinking about the end of time and the end of our own lives. They raise questions about the ultimate meaning of life and creation. Two unique Christian teachings about eschatology color the whole way we think about life in the here and now as well as the way we think about the future.

First, God's eschaton is *both* a present reality and a future hope. Bible scholars and theologians call this pattern, discerned from scripture, "already/not-yet" eschatology. Whatever is true about the eschaton is already a reality in the Christian life. At the same time, whatever is true about the eschaton is not yet here in its fullness.

Christians live in this tension, between the time of Jesus' resurrection and the time when he will come again. Already, Jesus has won victory over sin and death. Already, Jesus has risen from the grave. Already, Jesus offers us new life. Already, God's people are filled with the power of the Holy Spirit. Already, the church is doing God's work in the world. All of this already is a source of strength and confidence. It means that we have a real basis for courage and power.

At the same time, the world still suffers under the condition of sin. The truth that Christ is King is not yet visible to the whole world. Our lives are not yet fully transformed. Creation and society are still subject to the terrible effects of sin; babies still die of hunger, greed still trumps love, and we still weep at funerals. Between Christ's resurrection and the day when every knee will bow before him (Philippians 2:10), we need Christian hope for the not-yet-here future, hope that God has promised to wipe every tear from every eye (Revelation 7:17) and that God always keeps his promises.

The second key feature of biblical eschatology is that it is holistic. As Christians, our hope for the future is not that some part of us will be saved; it is that we will be saved as whole people. Not just souls, but bodies too, belong to God, and God promises that we will share a resurrection like Christ's. Christian hope is also hope for the material world, for the redemption of all creation. While we expect the world to be changed in God's future, we don't expect it to disappear. Christian hope is hope for a new heavens and a new earth (Revelation 21:1), and so all of creation is included in our hope. The holism of Christian hope leads us right to our first question in this chapter.

Does the world matter?

Maybe you've sung this in church: "This world is not my home." Or this: "I'll fly away, oh glory, I'll fly away." Stirring song lyrics, but, finally, not the best theology. Christian hope is not about escape from this life or this world; it is not about the soul "flying away" to heaven while leaving this earth behind.

Christians are sometimes accused of believing in "pie in the sky when you die" or of using Christian hope as a dangerous drug (Karl Marx infamously called religion "the opiate of the masses") to sedate people so they won't rebel against evil.[1] If Christians are using hope as a way to ignore this world, then we're not being faithful. The witness of Scripture is consistent from Genesis to Revelation. This world matters. It matters because God made it and called it good and because God is working to redeem it. To remember that *this* world and *this* life are good is one of the most Christian things we can do. An early challenge to Christian faith came from Gnostic groups who said that bodies and materiality were bad, that salvation was about escape. Against this, the early church insisted that our problem is not the world and our bodies. Our problem is sin. God will redeem us from sin, and redemption includes body and soul, heaven and earth. The overwhelming consensus of Christian readers of Scripture is that creation, at the eschaton, will be refined, not destroyed. God keeps his promises and redeems what he has made.

What happens to us when we die?

Well, we rot. Then, we wait in joyous anticipation of the general resurrection.

Death is the separation of the soul from the body. In death, a human being, intended by God to be a whole creature, is split in two. Body and soul are torn apart. Christians agree about what happens to bodies at that point. They are subject to decay. We bury the body or cremate it, and maybe we try not to think about it too much.

Christians are not in complete agreement about the condition of the soul at this point. If I die tomorrow, and Jesus returns ten years later, raising all his people to resurrected life, what is my condition for the ten years between my death and the great day of resurrection? This is the question of the "intermediate state." The majority Christian opinion is that the soul exists in a conscious intermediate state, enjoying God's presence while waiting to be reunited with the body in resurrection. This interpretation of Scripture makes sense of our common belief that those we love, who die in Christ, are in his presence. It also makes sense of key biblical evidence, most importantly the moment where Jesus tells the thief on the cross that "today" he will be with Jesus in paradise (Luke 23:43). Since neither Jesus nor the thief are resurrected on Good Friday, and since both of their bodies are definitely dead on that day, it makes sense to imagine "paradise" as a conscious life of the soul.

A minority Christian opinion, sometimes called "soul sleep," is that the soul, like the body, is bound by death, and that it will only return to life and consciousness at the general resurrection. This position, held by important thinkers including Martin Luther, makes sense of scriptural talk about the dead as "sleepers" (e.g., 1 Thessalonians 4:13). It also makes sense of the horror of death and the importance of our bodies. Notice that people who hold both positions agree that our ultimate hope is not for whatever happens on the day of death but for the general resurrection, when all humanity will share in the resurrection of Christ.

The most important answer to the question of what will happen after we die, then, is that we will be resurrected like Christ. Soul and body will be reunited. In 1 Corinthians 15, Paul talks about the resurrection of the body using the metaphor of a seed and the plant that will grow from it. When we die, our bodies are like seeds. At the resurrection, we will sprout, grow and be transformed into the likeness of Christ.

Paul's metaphor suggests that we can expect continuity between our bodies as we know them now and the resurrected bodies God promises us. Acorns are materially continuous with oak trees. Christian hope is not for souls to "fly away" when we die. It is hope for a future that is continuous with the present, hope for the bodies we have right now. Continuity between bodies now and resurrected bodies makes sense in light of Jesus' resurrection. The resurrected Jesus is materially continuous with the Jesus who died on the cross. The tomb is empty. He bears the scars of the crucifixion. He eats fish. The physicality of the resurrection characterizes Christian hope. This continuity is good news for us as believers. It means that our bodies now matter. They are the very stuff of our final salvation.

Paul's seed metaphor also shows us that we can expect discontinuity between our bodies now and resurrected bodies. The transition from acorn to oak tree involves serious transformation! Resurrection is not the reanimation of corpses. In resurrection, God does something new. Discontinuity between bodies now and resurrected bodies also makes sense when we think about Jesus' resurrection. The resurrected Jesus is materially transformed. He seems to pass through doors. Sometimes people recognize him, but sometimes they don't. He's changed (see Luke 24). This discontinuity is also good news because, now, under the condition of sin, our bodies are troubled. We get hurt. We die. We're frustrated by sinful desires. God promises that this trouble will be transformed.

As Paul puts it, "The body that is sown is perishable, it is raised imperishable; it is sown in dishonor, it is raised in glory; it is sown in weakness, it is raised in power; it is sown a natural body, it is raised a spiritual body" (1 Corinthians 15:42-44). It's important to notice that the changes between now and the resurrection day are *not* about escaping the body. Both the "natural body" and the "spiritual body" are bodies. The difference between now and the resurrection day is about being transformed from embodied-creatures-under-the-condition-of-sin, creatures who are selfish, to embodied-creatures-under-the-guidance-of-the-Holy-Spirit, creatures who "bear the image of the heavenly man" (1 Corinthians 15:49), the resurrected, embodied Jesus.

Do we become angels when we die?

No.

Angels and human beings are two different kinds of creatures. Humans have bodies, and angels don't.

Should we be happy that the dead are "in a better place"?

Paul counsels, "Brothers and sisters, we do not want you to be uninformed about those who sleep in death, so that you do not grieve like the rest of mankind, who have no hope. For we believe that Jesus died and rose again, and so we believe that God will bring with Jesus those who have fallen asleep in him" (1 Thessalonians 4:13-14). These words are sometimes used to suggest that Christians have no business grieving our dead, a suggestion that is often very hurtful to those who have lost a loved one. That suggestion also runs counter to what Paul says here and to the larger biblical witness.

Paul doesn't tell us not to grieve. He tells us not to grieve *in a certain way*, like those who "have no hope." It is natural and right to grieve our dead. Two biblical themes help us to see how this is the case. First, Scripture repeatedly shows us that human beings are very precious, both to God and to one another. Even given a conscious intermediate state, the loss of the body is a real loss. The death of a loved one is, indeed, terrible. Jesus wept at his friend's grave. Second, Scripture portrays death as the grievous result of sin. Death is not God's good will for us. It is an enemy, a defeated enemy to be sure, but it is still monstrous. Of course we weep when we commit our loved ones to the grave. We are separated from them. Their precious lungs no longer breathe; their precious hearts no longer beat.

The difference between Christians and those who have no hope, then, is not that Christians smile eerily in the face of death while the hopeless feel human pain. The difference, between Christians on the one hand and those who have no hope on the other, is hope itself. That hope is very specific; it is hope in Christ and his resurrection. We are free to grieve and to comfort the grieving, to recognize what we have lost, even while we trust and find consolation in the truth that death is not the end.

Is _____ a sign of the end times?

It's not uncommon to hear Christians suggest that some current event— such as the results of an election, a natural disaster—is a sign that the end is near. Is it? The best answer is probably both "yes" and "no." Better, the answer is first "no" and only then a careful, possible "yes."

For centuries, believers have been making dire end-time predictions. Some have crafted careful calendars, declaring the precise date of the end of the world. The antichrist figure has been identified as an ancient heretic named Arius, a variety of popes, and political leaders of many stripes. For centuries, believers making these overly confident predictions have been embarrassed, maybe even disappointed, to see the chosen dates come and go.

Scripture offers repeated warnings against arrogantly supposing that we know exactly what God is up to. About the eschaton, Jesus even tells us "about that day or hour no one knows, not even the angels in heaven, nor the Son, but only the Father" (Mark 13:32). Here, then, is a warning against trying to correlate this or that current event with the end of the world as we know it. Jesus himself doesn't (or, at least didn't during his life on earth) know the Father's timing. We'd have to be suffering a serious loss of humility to suppose that we know more than he did. This isn't all that Jesus has to say on the matter, and other parts of the Mark passage point to a more positive stance toward signs of the end:

> Be on guard! Be alert! You do not know when that time will come. It's like a man going away: He leaves his house and puts his servants in charge, each with their assigned task, and tells the one at the door to keep watch. "Therefore keep watch because you do not know when the owner of the house will come back—whether in the evening, or at midnight, or when the rooster crows, or at dawn." (Mark 13:33-35)

We don't know when the time will come, but that doesn't mean we're meant to relax into the here and now, falsely certain that the status quo will keep on going for countless millennia. Instead, we're supposed to be alert, eagerly watching and waiting for the Lord's return. We're to live like people who may be welcoming the king at any moment, always aware that God's future is just over the horizon. Here, without trying to correlate a specific current event with "end times," we are free to understand the suffering of the present time as a sign that the end is, indeed, coming. We live in eager expectation of the coming kingdom.

Pre-, Post-, What?

If you've heard talk about the "end times," you've probably also heard people throw around language like "pretrib" and "postmill." I've already argued that Christian hope is much larger than end times predictions, but to understand the conversation, at least in the North American church, we'll need some understanding of these terms.

Terms like *premillennialism* center around interpretation of the book of Revelation. Some Christians read it as full of historical references to the situation of the early church's suffering under the Roman Empire. Others read it as a series of future predictions about the second coming

Historic Premillennialism. This is the dominant position in Christian history. Christ will return *before* the thousand years referenced in Revelation 20. This theology expects Christians to share in sufferings before Christ returns, to greet Him as he returns to earth, and then to enjoy the kingdom with him. The resurrection of all humanity is emphasized.

Dispensational Premillennialism. This (sometimes, "dispensationalism") reads Revelation to indicate that, first, before a time of great tribulation, God will remove the faithful from the earth (a rapture). Then, Jesus will return and reign for a thousand years. Christians escape earth before they would have to undergo suffering.

Postmillennialism. This view expects the return of Christ to happen *after* the millennium, a time where Christ reigns from heaven through the power of the gospel. Postmillennial theology became less prevalent after the terrible wars of the twentieth century, which discouraged the progressive optimism that had often characterized the church earlier in that century.

Amillennialism. This interprets the millennium in Revelation, not as a future thousand years, but as a more symbolic reference to the very real kingdom reign of Christ. Amillennialism tends to avoid specific future predictions.

of Christ. Still others read it as a kind of theological poetry, pointing to real truth about past, present and future without making precise prophecies. Millennial theologies center especially on readings of Revelation 20:1-10, which references "a thousand years" in which Satan is bound and souls of the martyrs reign with Christ. The thousand years here are the "millennium" in question, and the "pre-" or "post-" refer to whether the second coming of Christ is expected before or after that millennium. Premillennialism expects life on earth to get worse before Christ returns and so is sometimes characterized as "pessimistic." Postmillennialism is often seen as "optimistic" because the expectation is that Christ will use the church to make things better and better here on earth, ushering in a golden age that will end with his visible return. Whatever a Christian's millennial theology, all eschatology affirms that the world matters, and so that eschatology has gone terribly wrong if it is used as an excuse for fatalism about evil or abuse of the earth. If millennial optimism or pessimism threatens to interfere with faithful discipleship, we know we have a problem.

Rapture practice?

I have a friend who grew up at a church where a teacher would yell "Rapture practice!" and the children would jump up and down with their hands in the air, looking to the sky. If you come from a particular kind of Christian tradition, you'll be familiar with jokes about empty spaces suggesting that the rapture has happened.

The idea of a "rapture" in which believers are caught up into heaven and disappear from the earth, the kind of rapture in some movies and books like *Left Behind*, depends on a particular and limited interpretation of 1 Thessalonians 4:16-17:

> For the Lord himself will come down from heaven, with a loud command, with the voice of the archangel and with the trumpet call of God, and the dead in Christ will rise first. After that, we who are still alive and are left will be caught up together with them in the clouds to meet the Lord in the air. And so we will be with the Lord forever.

In dispensational Premillennialism, the being "caught up . . . to meet the Lord in the air" has been read, together with texts from Daniel and Revelation, to point to an escape plan for believers. This reading is, at best, a small minority opinion in the history of Christianity. It does, however, seem to sell books and make scary movies.

How else might we read the text? Certainly, Paul is talking here about the resurrection of the body and the return of the king, the "second coming" of Christ. Bible scholars have pointed to a tradition in which, when the king came home, his people would run out to meet him. Having greeted the king, the citizens would march triumphantly back to the city with him. This suggests that Paul is thinking here, not of Christians being zapped away from the earth, but of Christians meeting Jesus as he returns from the clouds and then returning, with him, to the earth. The movement of "rapture" is not a movement up and out. It is more of a jump for joy followed by triumphant return to this earth, to worship God in all the goodness of the kingdom.

What do hell and judgment have to do with God's goodness and grace?

There is much about hell that is mysterious. In theology, sometimes this mystery is called "inscrutability," meaning that it belongs to God in a way that human beings cannot understand.

In Western Christianity, hell is most often understood as God's just punishment for sin. Key biblical passages, like Jesus' reference in Matthew 25:41 to "the eternal fire prepared for the devil and his angels" support the view that hell is real and terrible. Larger biblical themes about God's goodness and justice help us to glimpse how hell fits together with God's character. The God we meet when we read Scripture is a holy God. God is perfect love and divine goodness. Simply put, sin has no place alongside this love and goodness. Sin is terrible, and the punishment of hell fits with the nature of sin itself. Could God be truly good or really just if he looked the other way from evil? There is a strong sense in which the biblical teaching of God's judgment of sin is among the most comforting truths of Christian faith. Between the now and the eschaton, we expect to live with evil. We feel its horror. The promise that God will judge evil, that God will not allow it to stand, is a promise of justice and goodness.

There have always been minority reports about hell among Christians— those who suggest that hell is real but not unending (annihilationism), and those who emphasize moments in Scripture which point to the vastness of God's mercy to speculate that all people will finally be saved (universalism). While I believe that the majority view of hell as eternal

Julian of Norwich. Julian, a medieval mystic, points to God's eschatological love. Her words speak of an enormous confidence in God's loving handling of the future:

> From our point of view, there are many deeds evilly done and such great harm given that it seems to us that it would be impossible that ever it should come to a good end; and we look upon this, sorrowing and mourning because of it, so that we cannot take our ease in the joyful beholding of God . . . and the cause is this: that the use of our reason is now so blind, so lowly, and so stupid, that we cannot know the exalted, wondrous Wisdom, the Power, and the Goodness of the blessed Trinity. . . . He says, "Thou shalt see for thyself that all manner of thing shall be well," as if He said "Pay attention to this now, faithfully and trustingly; and at the last end thou shalt see it in fullness of joy." . . . I interpret a mighty comfort about all the deeds of our Lord God that are still to come.[2]

punishment for sin makes the best sense of the biblical texts and of God's goodness and justice, I also think it is worth attending to these minority voices as a reminder that God's justice—as we know it in Scripture and in Jesus Christ—is often surprising, and that God's goodness and mercy are greater than anything we can imagine. In faith, I find it enough to trust in God's goodness and mercy, to pray for the salvation of my friends and my enemies, and to find comfort in the promise that God will call evil what it is and that his goodness will finally reign.

What is the kingdom of God?

It has come and is coming in Jesus. It is heaven and earth; spiritual and material; past, present and future. Scripture uses different images for the kingdom: a mustard seed, a body, a vineyard, a city, a bride.

Contemporary theologians, trying to reclaim a strong teaching of the resurrection of the body and the redemption of all creation, increasingly

Charles Wesley. Charles Wesley's hymn connects Christian hope to the present life and the coming future, giving praise to God for his reign over both.

Rejoice, the Lord is King!
Your Lord and King adore,
Mortals give thanks, and sing,
And triumph evermore;

chorus:
Lift up your heart, lift up your voice,
Rejoice, again, I say, rejoice.

Jesus the Savior reigns,
The God of truth and love,
When he had purged our stains,
He took his seat above.
(chorus)

His kingdom cannot fail,
He rules o'er earth and heaven;
The keys of death and hell
Are to our Jesus given.
(chorus)

He all his foes shall quell,
Shall all our sins destroy,
And every bosom swell
With pure seraphic joy.
(chorus)

Rejoice in glorious hope,
Jesus the judge shall come;
And take his servants up
To their eternal home.
(chorus)[3]

suggest that kingdom life will involve the redemption and continuation of some of the activities of this life in which God is glorified. We're used to thinking about music this way, but other parts of our life together might also be taken up in God's eschaton—not just singing, perhaps, but also baking, architecture, painting and storytelling might be used in kingdom life to glorify the Father, Son and Holy Spirit. It makes sense to suggest that the new heavens and the new earth, like resurrected bodies, will be both continuous and discontinuous with earth and heaven as they are now.

When the Church is able, through the power of the Spirit, to glorify God beautifully, to witness to what Christ has done truthfully and to live together lovingly, we get a sneak peak of the kingdom. Kingdom reality is that reality—already and not-yet visible in this world—in which God's will *is* done, as we pray it will be done, when we follow Jesus' example for prayer.

NOTES

Preface

[1] Kevin Vanhoozer taught on Wheaton's faculty from 2009 to 2012 and today is at Trinity Evangelical Divinity School.

Chapter 1

[1] Alexander Roberts and James Donaldson, eds., *The Ante-Nicene Fathers*, vol. 3 (Grand Rapids: Eerdmans, 1973), p. 700.

[2] Dietrich Bonhoeffer, *Letters and Papers from Prison*, ed. Eberhard Bethge, enlarged edition (New York: Touchstone, 1997), pp. 280-82.

[3] Jefferson Bethke's video, www.youtube.com/watch?v=1IAhDGYlpqY.

[4] Todd M. Johnson and Kenneth R. Ross, eds., *Atlas of Global Christianity 1910-2010* (Edinburgh: Edinburgh University Press, 2009).

Chapter 2

[1] *St. Athanasius: Select Works and Letters*, series 2, vol. 4 of A Select Library of Nicene and Post-Nicene Fathers of the Christian Church, ed. Philip Schaff (Grand Rapids: Eerdmans, 1987), p. 552.

[2] Westminster Confession of Faith, I.4.

[3] B. B. Warfield, "The Biblical Idea of Inspiration," in *The Inspiration and Authority of the Bible* (Philipsburg, NJ: P & R Publishing, 1980).

[4] Herman Bavinck, *Reformed Dogmatics*, vol. 1, *Prolegomena* (Grand Rapids: Baker, 2003), pp. 435-48.

[5] Augustine, "Letter 82, to Jerome," in *Letters 1-99*, part 2, vol. 1 of *Works of Saint Augustine*, ed. John E. Rotelle (New York: New City Press, 2001), p. 316.

[6] The Chicago Statement on Biblical Inerrancy is also published as an appendix in Norman Geisler, ed., *Inerrancy* (Grand Rapids: Zondervan, 1980), pp. 493-504.

Chapter 3

[1] Joe R. Jones, *A Grammar of Christian Faith: Systematic Explorations in Christian Life and Doctrine* (Oxford: Rowan & Littlefield Publishers, 2002), p. 58.

[2] *Theos* means "God" in Greek; *logos* means "word" or "speech."

[3]Gregory of Nyssa, *On Not Three Gods to Ablabium*, 15-17, in *The Trinitarian Controversy*, ed. William G. Rusch (Philadelphia: Fortress Press, 1980), p. 155.

[4]Karl Barth, *Church Dogmatics*, IV/1 (London and New York: T & T International, 1961), pp. 204-5; see also I/1, pp. 351, 355-58; II/1, pp. 284ff.

[5]Gregory of Nazianzus, "Oration on Holy Baptism," *Orations*, 40.41, in *Nicene and Post-Nicene Fathers*, 2nd series, ed. Philip Schaff and Henry Wace (Peabody, MA: Hendrickson, 1996), 7:375.

[6]Gregory of Nyssa, *On Not Three Gods*, 21, pp. 156-57.

[7]Mary Daly, *Beyond God the Father: Toward a Philosophy of Women's Liberation* (Boston: Beacon Press, 1973), p. 19.

[8]Gregory of Nazianzus, *Fifth Theological Oration*, VII, in NPNF, 2nd series, 7:320.

[9]St. Basil the Great, *On the Holy Spirit*, 18.44, trans. David Anderson (New York: St. Vladimir's Seminary Press, 1980), p. 71.

[10]Garrett Green, "The Gender of God and the Theology of Metaphor," in *Speaking the Christian God: The Holy Trinity and the Challenge of Feminism*, ed. Alvin F. Kimel Jr. (Grand Rapids: Eerdmans, 1992), p. 60.

[11]Augustine, *On Christian Doctrine*, I.V.5., in NPNF, 1st series, 3:20.

Chapter 4
[1]*The Literal Meaning of Genesis* 1.19.39, in *On Genesis*, I/13, *The Works of Saint Augustine: A Translation for the 21st Century*, trans. Edmund Hill (Hyde Park, NY: New City Press, 2002), pp. 186-87.

Chapter 5
[1]Richard Dawkins, *The God Delusion* (New York: Houghton Mifflin Harcourt, 2006), p. 51.

[2]Diogenes Allen, *Three Outsiders: Pascal, Kierkegaard, Simone Weil* (Princeton, NJ: Caroline Press, 1983), p. 26.

[3]Ibid.

[4]*Baudelaire, His Prose and Poetry*, ed. T. R. Smith (New York: Boni & Liveright, 1919), p. 82.

[5]David Bentley Hart, "Tsunami and Theodicy," *First Things*, March 2005, www .firstthings.com/article/2007/01/tsunami-and-theodicy--27.

[6]Karl Barth, *The Word in This World: Two Sermons*, ed. Kurt I. Johanson, trans. Christopher Asprey (Vancouver, BC: Regent College Publishing, 2007), p. 35.

[7]Ibid., pp. 41-42.

[8]Fyodor Dostoyevsky, *The Brothers Karamazov*, trans. David McDuff (New York: Penguin, 2003), p. 321.

[9]Martin Luther King Jr., "Eulogy for the Martyred Children (1963)," in *A Testament of Hope: The Essential Writings and Speeches of Martin Luther King, Jr.*, ed. James Washington (New York: HarperCollins, 1986), p. 221.

[10]C. S. Lewis, *The Screwtape Letters* (San Francisco: HarperCollins, 2001), pp. 160-61.

[11]"Family Tragedy," Library of Congress exhibition, www.loc.gov/exhibits/american colony/amcolony-family.html.

[12]Lausanne Theology Working Group, "A Statement on the Prosperity Gospel," Akropong, Ghana, October 8-9, 2008, and September 1-4, 2009, www.lausanne.org/en/documents/all/twg/1099-a-statement-on-the-prosperity-gospel.html.

[13]John Calvin, *Institutes of the Christian Religion*, 3.8.1, ed. John McNeill, trans. Ford Lewis Battles (Philadelphia: Westminster Press, 1960), p. 702.

[14]Fleming Rutledge, *The Undoing of Death* (Grand Rapids: Eerdmans, 2002), p. 236.

Chapter 7

[1]Unless otherwise indicated, all Scripture references in this chapter are from the NRSV.

Chapter 8

[1]*Spirit and Power: A 10-Country Survey of Pentecostals*, The Pew Forum on Religion & Public Life (2006), www.pewforum.org/files/2006/10/pentecostals-08.pdf.

[2]John Wesley, "Self Denial," §2.6, in *Sermons II*, ed. Albert C. Outler, vol. 2 of *The Bicentennial Edition of the Works of John Wesley* (Nashville: Abingdon, 1976), p. 247.

[3]John Wesley, "On Divine Providence," §16, in *Works*, 2:542.

[4]Charles Wesley, "Come, Holy Ghost, Our Hearts Inspire," in *The United Methodist Hymnal* (Nashville: United Methodist Publishing House, 1989), p. 603.

Chapter 9

[1]*The Persuaders: Americans Are Swimming in a Sea of Messages,* directed by Barak Goodman and Rachel Dretzin, written by Barak Goodman and Douglas Rushkoff (WGBH Educational Foundation, 2004), DVD. Online version: www.pbs.org/wgbh/pages/frontline/shows/persuaders.

[2]Quotes are from ibid.

[3]Unless otherwise indicated, all Scripture references in this chapter are from the NRSV.

[4]Martin Luther, "Letter to Philip Melanchthon from Wartburg August 1, 1521," in *Letters I*, ed. and trans. Gottfried G. Krodel; vol. 48 of Luther's Works, American edition, ed. Jaroslav Pelikan and Helmut T. Lehmann (Philadelphia: Fortress, 1963), p. 282.

[5]*The Heidelberg Catechism, 1563–1963*, 400th anniversary ed. (New York: United Church Press, 1962), pp. 9-11.

Chapter 10

[1]In Alexander Roberts, James Donaldson, A. Cleveland Coxe and Allan Menzies,

eds., Ante-Nicene Fathers: The Writings of the Fathers Down to A.D. 325, vol. 5 (Peabody, MA: Hendrickson Publishers, 1994), p. 384.

[2]John Calvin, *Institutes of the Christian Religion*, 4.1.1 and 4.1.4, ed. John McNeill, trans. Ford Lewis Battles (Philadelphia: Westminster Press, 1960), pp. 1011, 1016.

[3]Faith and Order Commission of the World Council of Churches, *Baptism, Eucharist and Ministry*, Faith and Order Paper No. 111 (Geneva, Switzerland: WCC, 1982).

[4]Ibid., under "Ministry," II.A.14.

[5]Michael O. Emerson and Christian Smith, *Divided by Faith: Evangelical Religion and the Problem of Race in America* (New York: Oxford University Press, 2000).

[6]Lausanne Movement homepage, www.lausanne.org/en, accessed June 5, 2013.

[7]"Christian Social Responsibility," The Lausanne Covenant, www.lausanne.org/en/documents/lausanne-covenant.html.

Chapter 11

[1]"Obama's Lead Among Younger Millennials Widens to 16 Points," Public Religion Research Institute, October 4, 2012, http://publicreligion.org/newsroom/2012/10/news-release-millennial-values-voter-engagement-2012.

[2]James W. Skillen, "Politics for Government, or Politics for Politics?" *Prism*, September/October 1994, pp. 16-20.

[3]Martin Luther King Jr., "Letter from Birmingham Jail," in *The Atlantic Monthly*, 212, no. 2 (1963): 78-88, www.uscrossier.org/pullias/wp-content/uploads/2012/06/king.pdf.

[4]Quoted in Albert Hsu, *Singles at the Crossroads* (Downers Grove, IL: InterVarsity Press, 1997), p. 178.

Chapter 12

[1]Karl Marx, *Critique of Hegel's Philosophy of Right*, ed. Joseph O'Malley (Cambridge: Cambridge University Press, 1970), p. 131.

[2]Fr. John-Julian OJN, ed., *The Complete Julian of Norwich* (Brewster, MA: Paraclete Press, 2009), p. 163.

[3]Charles Wesley, Hymn 8, *Resurrection Hymns* (1746), http://divinity.duke.edu/sites/default/files/documents/cswt/35_Resurrection_Hymns_%281746%29_Mod.pdf.

WHERE DO WE GO FROM HERE?

Basic Introductions

Grenz, Stanley J., David Guretzki and Cherith Fee Nordling, eds. *Pocket Dictionary of Theological Terms*. Downers Grove, IL: InterVarsity Press, 1999.

This is an outstanding pocket dictionary of theological terms that will define almost every technical word or phrase you need to know. Written for the beginning student.

Kapic, Kelly M. *A Little Book for New Theologians: Why and How to Study Theology*. Downers Grove, IL: IVP Academic, 2012.

Written by a skilled teacher of theology, this deeply practical and pastoral book discusses why we study theology and what benefits and pitfalls lay before us spiritually.

Olson, Roger E. *The Mosaic of Christian Belief: Twenty Centuries of Unity & Disunity*. Downers Grove, IL: InterVarsity Press, 2002.

Widely used as a textbook for college students, Olson's outline of theology not only covers the major categories in detail but diplomatically shows us the variety of positions Christians have taken on each issue. Olson's book can be ideally paired with this book, Theology Questions Everyone Asks.

Stott, John R. W. *Basic Christianity*. Downers Grove, IL: InterVarsity Press, 2008.

This is a classic, simple evangelical statement of Christian belief that has served generations of students since about 1960. Christian publishers often list it among the best Christian books of the twentieth century.

Wright, N. T. *Simply Christian: Why Christianity Makes Sense*. New York: HarperOne, 2006.

This is a celebrated, brief volume written for beginning students and church members who have never really thought about theological concepts before. It is easy to read and compelling and can be supplemented with a DVD showing Wright discussing each theme for group discussion.

Intermediate Studies

Allison, C. FitzSimons. *The Cruelty of Heresy: An Affirmation of Christian Orthodoxy*. Harrisburg, PA: Morehouse, 1994.

Boyd, Gregory A., and Paul R. Eddy. *Across the Spectrum: Understanding Issues in Evangelical Theology.* Second edition. Grand Rapids: Baker Academic, 2009.

Dyrness, William A., and Veli-Matti Kärkkäinen, eds. *Global Dictionary of Theology.* Downers Grove, IL: IVP Academic, 2008.

Elwell, W., ed. *The Evangelical Dictionary of Theology.* Grand Rapids: Baker Academic, 2001.

González, Justo L. *Essential Theological Terms.* Louisville: Westminster John Knox, 2005.

Hastings, Adrian, Alistair Mason and Hugh Pyper. *The Oxford Companion to Christian Thought: Intellectual, Spiritual, and Moral Horizons of Christianity.* Oxford: Oxford University Press, 2000.

Larsen, Timothy, and Daniel J. Treier, eds. *The Cambridge Companion to Evangelical Theology.* Cambridge: Cambridge University Press, 2007.

MacCullouch, Diarmaid. *Christianity: The First Three Thousand Years.* New York: Penguin, 2009.

McFarland, Ian A., David A. S. Fergusson, Karen Kilby and Iain R. Torrance, eds. *The Cambridge Dictionary of Christian Theology.* Cambridge: Cambridge University Press, 2011.

McGrath, Alister E. *Christian Theology: An Introduction.* Fifth edition. Oxford: Wiley-Blackwell, 2010.

Migliore, Daniel L. *Faith Seeking Understanding: An Introduction to Christian Theology.* Second edition. Grand Rapids: Eerdmans, 2004.

Noll, Mark A. *Jesus Christ and the Life of the Mind.* Grand Rapids: Eerdmans, 2011.

Olson, Roger. *The Story of Christian Theology.* Downers Grove, IL: InterVarsity Press, 1999.

Placher, William C., and Derek R. Nelson. *A History of Christian Theology: An Introduction.* Second edition. Louisville: Westminster John Knox, 2013.

Plantinga, Cornelius. *Engaging God's World: A Christian Vision of Faith, Learning and Living.* Grand Rapids: Eerdmans, 2002.

Williams, Rowan. *Tokens of Trust: An Introduction to Christian Belief.* Louisville: Westminster John Knox, 2007.

Finding the Texbook You Need

The IVP Academic Textbook Selector
is an online tool for instantly finding the IVP books
suitable for over 250 courses across 24 disciplines.

---

www.ivpress.com/academic/textbookselector